Jacqueline James was born in Birmingham into a family of gifted businessmen and entrepreneurs on the one side and psychics and musicians on the other. After obtaining a degree in History from London University, she worked in a variety of occupations including waitress, secretary, research assistant, sales administrator, and manager. She had resisted her own psychic ability for many years but realised its potential to help people to change their lives for the better during a stay of several months in Andalucia, southern Spain. It was here that she began to develop her techniques before finally settling down to use them professionally when her first child was born 16 years ago.

She now lives in Oxford with her family.

Take Control of Your Life

And See the Future Change in Your Hands

Jacqueline James

Hodder & Stoughton

Illustrations by Rodney Paul

British Library Cataloguing in Publication Data

James, Jacqueline
Take Control of your Life: and See the
Future Change in Your Hands
I. Title
133.6

ISBN 0 340 63844 3

Typeset by Palimpsest Book Production Limited,
Polmont, Stirlingshire
Printed and bound in Great Britain by
Cox and Wyman Ltd, Reading, Berkshire

Hodder and Stoughton
A division of Hodder Headline PLC
338 Euston Road
London NW1 3BH

Contents

Author's Note

Although permission was given to include the personal stories in this book, names and certain details have been changed to protect identity.

1

Take Control of Your Life

This book is going to show you how to get what you really want out of life.

Your hands hold the key to your future. Each line on them shows just where you are at this moment in time and the directions you are likely to take. Of course, you hope that the future will be good, but hoping is merely the start. Your fate is not completely predestined: you can change it. You can take control and begin to chart a course that will bring you more fulfilment, more prosperity, more love and more fun. But first of all you have to understand the thoughts and impulses that are driving you, and where they have come from.

Understanding Your Thoughts

Your hands are an exact mirror of what is going on in your head. Every thought you think ends up as a nervous impulse felt throughout your body, and persistently held thoughts result in the lines on your hands and affect the shape of your fingers. You are, in fact, continuously creating your own future and you can change it. Change your thoughts and you will change your future and your hands will change.

Why we get into ruts

Your genetic inheritance has given you your colouring,

size, shape and brain power. These form the bedrock of who you are. However, from birth you are also exposed to powerful influences in your family background, your relationships and the world around you, and together these shape your unique outlook on life, for example whether you feel good or depressed. Whatever your frame of mind, though, you seem to have little or no control over it.

We also absorb certain key ideas from society. The majority of us seem to have taken on board attitudes like believing that:

- You have to work hard in order to make ends meet
- You're lucky to have a job
- The real riches are for the privileged few only
- A certain number of years are allotted to you and then your body just packs up and dies
- Romantic love is fleeting
- With the divorce rate rocketing, your chances of lasting happiness are slim

Religion, too, has taught us to believe that wanting things is greedy and undesirable, that it is good to be poor, to suffer patiently in difficult relationships. Although in the latter half of the twentieth century many of these concepts are being overthrown, they still sit at the bottom of our consciousness, thwarting our progress.

The truth is, such ideas lead us astray. What we need are the means that will enable us to strip away unproductive and harmful thinking and start programming our thoughts to create the things we really want.

Why we want the things we want (and why we should have them)

We all have deep longings that just won't go away. No matter how much circumstances might thwart us or make our desires seem downright impossible, these longings keep surfacing, reminding us that we are not where we truly want to be. If we continue to ignore them, an all-pervasive 'deadness' enters our lives.

Nevertheless, we are surrounded by conflict. On the one hand, we see daily on our televisions and in the newspapers the massive poverty and strife in other parts of the world. We see innocent children starving to death. In this context, our desires for more comfort and wealth seem downright greedy and inappropriate. On the other hand, these same newspapers and televisions bombard us daily with advertisements and stories encouraging us to want luxury.

Neither of these should thwart our own directions in life. If we want something deeply, it is because some aspect of our own creativity and personality needs it for growth and fulfilment; it is by developing ourselves through the pursuit of these desires that the world develops and is enhanced.

The world is full of possibilities – more than we have yet dreamed of. These possibilities can only be realised through our creativity. The world needs us to want progress; it is part of being human and it is the way we were designed to be so that the world and everything in it can grow.

Even studies of quantum physics suggest that our human consciousness is participating in the creation of the universe rather than the other way round. By making contact with our intuitive selves through doing the exercises in this book, we can avoid making mistakes for ourselves, others or the planet. As we heal our own lives, we are also healing part of the tissue of the planet; healing ourselves means recognising that our lives were meant to be abundant, creative and free.

In this book, I am going to put the principles of palmistry in reverse. I propose to show you how you can take control of your thoughts in such a way that the lines on your hands will change and your future will be transformed for the better.

Some of you may only be interested in certain chapters, such as health, love, or money and prosperity, and the book is arranged so that you can work only on these if you prefer. However, some of the exercises given for other chapters may be helpful as well, so it is a good idea to go through them when you have time.

Above all, realise that your life is full of possibilities. As you start to see results, your goals and ideas will start to change and you will begin to grow even more. You will be surprised that your life could change so much and that you have achieved all this yourself.

Understanding Your Hands

For centuries the palm has been used as a means of 'predicting' the future, but in our scientific, technological world it has been discredited as belonging to the realms of fantasy. In certain scientific circles, principally in Russia and Germany, however, research has shown that lines and patterns on the hands reveal the beginnings of certain diseases, and that with preventative treatment, those patterns will either diminish or vanish altogether. The head line, for example, is used as an indicator to paediatricians of possible neurological disturbances in babies; and studies at the University of Munich have shown that they are able to predict with 80 per cent accuracy a newborn's chances of developing specific diseases.

Further studies have examined the traditional meanings of the lines in relation to the actual occurrences in a person's life, for example comparing the lifeline with the length of a person's life, the head line with brain power and career patterns, the heart line with the strength of the organ itself and the emotions, the affection lines with someone's love life, and so on.

To begin with, most of the data simply noted that as people's lives changed, whether as the result of trauma or a sudden decision to leave a job or a partner, for example, the lines on their hands also changed. It was a logical extension of this to see if the patterns of thinking that were causing frustration or unhappiness and were being reflected in the lines on the person's hands could be changed by certain techniques such as affirmation, creative visualisation and so on. The answer was yes, with the result that once the patterns of both thoughts and lines had changed, a traditional palmist would be able to predict a different and very much better future.

In this book I will be giving a brief explanation of the traditional meanings of the hands in relation to the important areas of your life – health, wealth, longevity, work and love – and then some techniques and exercises that will enable you to get your life moving in the directions you really want. As you work on these exercises, the lines on your hands will begin to change. Some will lengthen and deepen, some will break up, fade, or disappear entirely.

The amount of time this takes depends on the strength of the thoughts that created the lines in the first place. If unproductive patterns of thinking are very deeply rooted in your psyche there can be a strong period of resistance to change and naturally the hands will reflect this. Nevertheless, once you have stimulated your thought patterns to create new directions for your future, progress is absolutely assured, and the lines on your hands will be the visible signs by which you can measure your success.

For example, one man had a long lifeline on his left hand and a short one on his right, indicating that although he was programmed to live to a good age, he had gradually come to believe that he would not, and this was beginning to affect his health. His father, grandfather and two uncles had all died young and he had become convinced that he would follow suit. It took several months of gentle but consistent reprogramming before the lifeline on his right hand developed a branch line that swung out from the old line to create a new path and his health improved.

Lines of creativity or intuition, however, often respond quite quickly – sometimes within a matter of weeks – once the required changes have been made. Say, for example, that you have had a long-cherished ambition for your career but for various reasons have never made any real attempt to get if off the ground or perhaps have been thwarted. Once you start to work on getting what you really want, the significant lines will rapidly develop or strengthen.

General palmistry principles

Although there is continual debate about the meanings of the right and left hands – the gypsies, for example, only ever look at the left hand as being nearest to the heart – I have found that the differences between them are in line with general biological and psychological principles. The left hand corresponds to the right hemisphere of the brain and represents your feeling, imaginative, intuitive side. The lines on the left hand also show the patterns and programming that come from your genetic inheritance and family background.

The right hand corresponds to the left hemisphere of the brain governing your thinking, rational, logical self. It also shows how you are dealing with the hand that fate has dealt you. In other words, it shows whether you are making a better or worse job of what you were given as a start in life.

If you are left-handed it means that you tend to give emphasis to the intuitive side of the brain, and both hands must be read to determine to what degree your lines have accommodated this.

So now you are probably looking at your hands, their shape and the lines on them, and wondering what it all means. But before we even begin to look at this we need to get right down to what you really want in your life. You can't make changes until your mind is clear about the goals you are aiming at.

Getting Started Right Now

With one or two simple exercises you are going to uncover those desires lying hidden deep in your psyche. You are going to let your imagination roam free.

Step 1 Take a piece of paper and at the top write: *If money and circumstance were no obstacle I would . . .* List everything you would really love to do, or have, no matter how impossible they seem.

If you have limited yourself for a long time, you may at first have difficulty thinking of things, but stick at it until you feel you are expressing what you truly want. Then look at your list and select at least one thing you can do right now – and *do it*.

Maybe you've longed to go down to the coast for the day but have talked yourself out of it for practical reasons.

Maybe you'd love to take an unauthorised day off work because you're sick of it. Taking the day off could be just what you need to see the rut you've dug for yourself.

You want to go to Paris, Hawaii, the Edinburgh Festival, spend some time in the country, go winter sporting, attend the opera once a month, become a pop groupie.

You want a new car, new curtains, a new house, a new outfit.

You have a long-cherished ambition to start your own business; to express yourself creatively through painting, dance, music or writing; to renovate cars, get into antiques; to start a new trend in some cherished project.

Take your project off the back burner and do something about it. Get the brochures, book the tickets, buy some clothes or tools, enrol in the creative class, start the business, begin the project. These aims and ambitions are unique to you. They represent your true self trying to be born.

If the things you have written seem too big to achieve right now, do something smaller towards it. For example, you may want a new carpet but feel that it is too big a financial outlay at the moment. See if buying a rug would be a compromise by giving you a new floor covering to go on top of your old carpet but would not stretch your resources so much.

If you would like to start your own business and are worried about the risk, test the water first by keeping your job and trying out your projects in the evenings or at weekends.

Taking action like this stimulates your creative mind to come up with more and better ideas. Sometimes it can lead to the abandonment of one project because an entirely new opportunity presents itself.

Step 2   On another piece of paper write about your life as you see it at the moment. Make a list of all your feelings, doubts and hopes and really try to understand and express how you feel about your life right now. Keep writing for several minutes.

Step 3   Compare the list from step 1 with what you have just written. List 1 is almost certainly all positive and full of possibilities. It represents where you want to go. List 2 shows you where you are now. It probably has a few doubts in it; maybe even many. You now have to build a bridge that will take you from list 2, your starting point, to list 1, your goals.

Step 4   Look at how many negative statements you have made on list 2. For example, if you are really low, your list may begin something like this:

'Nothing works. My job is awful. I can't seem to make ends meet and have enough money left over to save up for that trip to the Greek Islands. My love life is only mediocre.'

Such negative statements represent the doubts that are holding you back from your goal. However, *they are not real*. They are only thoughts stemming from negative feelings, and they can be changed.

Now you need to turn each negative statement from your list into a positive one. Use the present tense. Your subconscious mind acts in the present and you therefore need to give it clear instructions, for example:

- I am now making the adjustments to make everything work much better

- I am beginning to see the best in my job and am attracting something better right now
- I am now beginning to create and attract a surplus in my finances and my holiday money is quickly growing
- My love life is improving right now

As you write these statements, you are probably feeling quite a lot of resistance. Your mind doesn't want to give up its cherished views and will reason you out of believing anything different. This is why we are going to help it change with *visualisation*.

Step 5 There will be other more specific visualisation exercises later on, but the following will help you get started on bridging these two lists.

Sit down or lie comfortably. Make sure that you are warm, using a blanket, duvet or sleeping bag if necessary.

Close your eyes and begin to breathe deeply, counting to three as you breathe in, and three as you breathe out.

When you feel relaxed, count slowly backwards from ten down to one, relaxing your muscles more deeply with each number.

When you reach one, you should be fairly relaxed. Don't worry if still you feel tension somewhere. The important thing is that you are as relaxed as you can be at this moment. Each moment in your life is the only moment that matters. It contains everything you are. It is the moment where you experience life.

Now take your mind to the things you wrote in list 1, the things you really would love if you could have them, or the positive affirmations you made at the end of list 2. See yourself with those things. See yourself enjoying them. The sun is shining and life is good. Everyone likes you. Just absorb the enjoyment of it all. Allow yourself the luxury of wallowing in the pleasure of these things.

Now, very gently take one of the images and move it to the right of your mind's eye. This is the thing that you want. Let's suppose, for example, that it is the sum of £1,000.

Now move your attention to the left of your mind's eye and see there your current situation. Let us suppose that you are broke, so you have zero on the left and £1,000 on the right.

Don't worry if you lose the image, or can hardly visualise it at all; if all you can see is a grey nothingness. Most of us do to begin with. Your intention is all that matters.

Now gently bring these two images – or ideas if you've lost the pictures – together into the centre of your mind. Merge them, and gently focus your attention on the image you want – in this case £1,000.

Breathe deeply and *know* that you have begun to create the change. Then gently open your eyes.

Research has shown that the brain 'sees' time as flowing from left to right so that by putting the image of what you want on the right and your current position on the left you are giving your mind the experience of what you want in the future to replace your current situation. And by bringing them together you are exercising your brain to overlay the present picture with the future one; you are therefore bridging the two hemispheres of the brain.

You can use this technique as often or as little as you like, but if you are really serious, a few minutes early each morning or before you go to bed for twenty-eight days (the moon's cycle) is ideal. However, I have known people who have begun to notice the beginnings of change within ten days or so.

You may not achieve your goal in quite the way you want at this stage. The ability to move yourself out of your habitual-thinking rut towards clarity and creativity will improve with practice, and all the techniques in this book will help to exercise you in different ways. The main thing at this point is that as soon as things start to move, you will begin to realise that you are in control of what is coming to you.

If your goal was £1,000 and you get an extra £50, say, you must still give yourself a pat on the back for managing to create that amount. Those first achievements are the stepping stones to greater ones. The more you keep at it, the faster and easier it becomes. Ignore any doubts and press on. You have just opened the door to change.

2

Take Control of Your Prosperity

'The most fruitful of all the arts is the art of living well'

Cicero

By prosperity I mean not simply money and the things it can buy, but that sense of wellbeing which acts as a magnet for good fortune, friendship and happiness. In fact the relationship between attitude and prosperity is a vital one.

In our society based on the anaesthetising effects of the welfare state, many of us have lost that hunger to break out and carve a unique path for ourselves. We tend to accept the established order of things and end up working forty hours a week for a wage that just about covers the basic necessities. We grow up with ideas such as:

'Money doesn't grow on trees.'
'A poor man is an honest man.'
'Hard work never killed anyone.'
'You never get rich on a wage so what's the point.'
'As long as I've got enough to get by.'
'We can't all be rich.'
'There are limits to everything.'

All this is very worthy but as human beings we were never intended to strain ourselves to the limit to make ends meet. A large majority of the population has tied itself up in knots with hard work and stress and many people believe that a prosperous life is beyond them unless they win a lottery or the pools.

Reading Your Hands

To determine your own attitudes towards money and prosperity, or the lack of it, check the third phalange of your fingers, that is, the one nearest the knuckle. Before we begin, however, it is important to note that your hands don't have to reveal problems for the techniques described in this book to work. They will bring improvements whatever your situation.

A good sign is if the phalange is full and balanced with the other two phalanges, giving the fingers a clear line (fig. 2.1). If this is the case on both hands, it means that you have a healthy respect for money and it flows more or less easily in your life. You could even be wealthy.

The first sign of minor trouble is when the third phalanges of your left hand are fairly full and balanced but the right ones are shorter or are narrow and 'wasp-waisted' (fig. 2.2). If your right hand looks like this it means that you probably started out with an open mind but

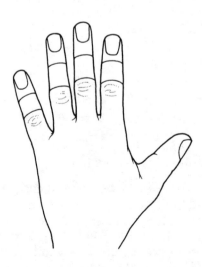

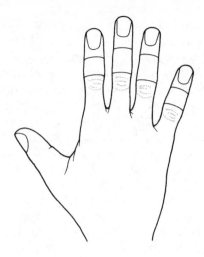

your experiences have led it to become ingrained with negative thoughts about money, perhaps that:

- It is hard to come by
- It goes out faster than it comes in
- It is an endless slog just to make ends meet
- You'll never be rich
- A wage means just about keeping my head above water, and so on

Your balanced left hand shows that you were born with the potential to get what you want materially. Perhaps yours was a secure and comfortable background, or maybe you always 'knew' that your life should be developing in a comfortable and prosperous way. Somewhere along the line, however, life became difficult, with bills to pay and the things you wanted beyond your means. A negative, downward spiral began. You started to tell yourself that life is hard and money is in short supply. Your right hand has begun to reflect your doubts.

Well, you can change it back again.

A much more problematical configuration indicating problems concerning money is short or wasp-waisted, narrow third phalanges on *both* hands.

In this case, you grew up with the idea that there is not enough money to go round, and that in the prosperity stakes you drew the short straw. This could be the result of a childhood affected by poverty, or perhaps yours was a comfortably-off home but you still felt that you couldn't have what you wanted. Maybe your ancestors had a hard financial struggle and it is in your genes to feel this way.

People from poor or difficult backgrounds can even keep this configuration after they have married into considerable comfort and wealth, and I have seen this many times. They cannot give themselves permission to enjoy their good fortune because they haven't created the wealth themselves. Their negative attitude towards money is ingrained and they haven't had to change their thinking.

I have, however, also seen wonderfully balanced patterns on the hands of people who have suffered appalling difficulties and poverty. The very lack of money and comfort has been the spur that has propelled them upwards.

Carol, for example, was brought up in a children's home, left school without any qualifications, married at sixteen and had four children in as many years. The marriage was hopeless and he walked out on her when she was twenty-three.

Today, at the age of forty-two, she has two successful hairdressing and beauty businesses, two luxurious homes – one in England, the other in Spain – drives a Mercedes Benz and has a first-class honours degree in philosophy from Birkbeck College in London. She is currently planning to open another salon and work towards her doctorate.

Carol's achievements are particularly wonderful because she started with nothing and was strong-minded enough to fight for herself. No one loved her enough as a child for her to want to absorb their thought patterns. In her childhood world she saw only an institution and people she knew were nothing to do with her.

In the outside world she saw shops and cosmetics and beautiful salesgirls and she made her own rules. She wanted all that beauty and glitter for herself. No one she respected had ever told her that she couldn't have it, or that it might be hard and that she could be wasting her time, because nobody cared. She programmed her own mind – just as you can programme yours. When you do so, the muscles around your hands and fingers will relax and the third phalange will appear to lengthen or will fill out.

The following exercises, which should be started after you have gone through the basic exercises outlined on pp. 7–11, will put you on the road to success.

The Beginnings of Change

To change your financial situation you have to change your thoughts. Since babyhood, every single thought and idea you have had or been exposed to has registered in your memory and even though you may have forgotten a lot of them, they are still there, steadily ticking away in your consciousness and affecting how much money you think you can have. If you want to change your financial situation, you are going to have to change your way of thinking. Here's how.

Set yourself goals

A recent survey of self-made millionaires shows that not one of them came to be so rich by accident. They all knew they were aiming to be millionaires. This is the key: to set yourself goals, not limits.

Step 1 – Getting started The only place you can start is exactly where you are now. Assess your current situation by asking yourself these three questions:

- Are you happy with the amount of money in your life?
- Do you have enough income?
- Do you have enough capital, savings or investments?

Unless you are a millionaire or a religious person dedicated to poverty, I doubt the answer to any of these is yes.

So take a deep breath, and here we go: you are going to become richer.

Step 2 – Goal Setting   Like any self-made person, you have to set goals for yourself. You must have an action plan to guide your ideas.

Take a piece of paper and write on it:

1 An amount of money that you would like to receive within a fairly short space of time, say three to six months. This must be in addition to what you would normally expect from your job or savings. The amount should seem relatively feasible.
2 How much you would like to be worth in eighteen months to two years' time. This amount should be more than you feel is really possible for you without being completely outrageous.
3 An outrageous, apparently impossible amount of money. The kind of money you see in your wildest dreams. Give yourself a longer time span, say five years.

If your resistance is high, the chances are you will say this is rubbish, what can this possibly achieve? If you are open, however, you will probably be surprised to think that you want such things, let alone that you might have them.

Step 3 – Reviewing   Every few days or so, and at least once a week, you need to read through your goals to see if they need adjusting. Perhaps they are uncomfortably high at the moment, or maybe not quite high enough.

Also, as you try the exercises below, you will experience changes and improvements and it is important to acknowledge this. Quite often goals are achieved in unexpected ways and are not immediately seen as achievements. For example, you might receive a tax rebate or find a way of doing something that makes substantial savings. One woman achieved her goal of an extra £1,000 in three months by moving her horse to a cheaper and more suitable livery yard. It was only when she was totting up all her bills that she realised the £1,000 was already in the bank because she hadn't needed to spend it.

Here are several techniques to help you open your mind to being creative so that you can pull towards you those things you want.

Affirmations

This is one of the most effective techniques for making significant changes. Affirmations are positive statements which gradually fill your mind with the idea of success and replace the old negative thinking that has been holding you back.

At first these affirmations may seem like the lines children used to have to write at school. Indeed, the process is apparently so simple you will probably experience some resistance. Ours isn't a culture that encourages easy ways out of working hard, but this process does just that.

Step 1   Take a large piece of paper, turn it horizontally and draw a line down the middle. In the left-hand column, list and number all your feelings about money, especially your feelings about achieving some of the goals you have made. Include any ideas you may have picked up from family or friends such as:

'Money doesn't grow on trees.'
'You must put money by for a rainy day.'

'You must start thinking about your pension.'
'With all this unemployment you're lucky even to have a job.'

Try hard to delve down and get at those thoughts that leave you feeling helpless.

My biggest problem thought was that wealth is vulgar and scrimping and saving virtuous, but yours may be different. The important thing is to contact those feelings that are driving your actions.

Step 2   When your list feels complete – and it may be quite short – start at the top of the right-hand column and alongside your first statement write down an affirmation to counteract it. For example:

Left	Right
I'll never be rich because my job doesn't pay enough	I can be rich whether I work or not
Money doesn't grow on trees	Money can be found in all sorts of unusual places
I can't become wealthy doing the things I love	I can become wealthy doing whatever I like

If you are doing this seriously, you will certainly be feeling something – most likely disbelief, possibly irritation and maybe even cynical dismissal. Hang in there. These feelings are the very ones that have stopped you getting where you want to be. The next step may seem tedious, but it is the foundation stone for rebuilding the thoughts that will bring you what you really want.

Step 3   Choose one or two of the affirmations from the right-hand column – the ones that 'resonate' most strongly for you – and on another piece of paper write them out at least six times (psychologists have discovered that the mind is most receptive to new ideas after six repetitions). You must use your *first name* and you must use the *present tense* as the subconscious only accepts ideas in

the present. If you say 'I *will* do something,' it is a signal
to your subconscious to switch off until a later date. For
example one of my key affirmations is: 'Wealth comes
to me, Jackie, from new and exciting sources. I, Jackie,
do not need to work.'

At first, repeatedly writing out that I didn't need to work
made me feel both upset and light-headed. I had always
been so conscientious, a right little goody two-shoes. But
I was also heartily cheesed off with having no time for
the things that I really wanted to do, so I decided to go
for it. Results began to be seen within a few months, as
I shall explain later, and today I am living the life I've
always wanted.

Similarly, as you write these statements you may notice
a lot of resistance in yourself. You may be thinking 'This
is rubbish. This will never get me anywhere.' Make a
note of these contradictions and at the end of your list of
affirmations, just write three or four times an affirmation
which turns it into a positive thought. For example, say
you are writing:

'I can leave my present job and become abundantly
wealthy,'

and you start to feel:

'Oh yes, and pigs might fly,'

or

'Other people might be able to but I can't,'

or

'It's just plain impossible,'

or

'It's all a load of old rubbish. Nothing works for me.'

All of these can be turned into positive statements, for
example:

'Pigs might not fly, but I can certainly become
wealthy.'

'I can be as successful as the wealthiest person.'

'Nothing is impossible.'

'I now choose to treat affirmations seriously.'

'Everything works for me when I try.'

Repeat the whole of Step 3 for about a week or until

you begin to feel that a change has been made or that you have done enough. Early morning or before you go to bed are good times to write down your affirmations, but you can do it whenever you feel like it. Once a day is enough, but if you feel like more, all the better.

Don't be alarmed if some things appear to go wrong, for example you mislay some money. This is a sure sign that you are shaking up your mental processes. As you persevere, financial improvements will begin to follow.

The results of affirmations

One woman, a single mother, was working as a clerical assistant in a hospital and supporting – with difficulty – her family of four. After studying part-time, she had gained her ITEC massage qualification, but had 'sat' on it for two years. Then she started making affirmations, and within a matter of weeks she had begun to take a few private clients for massage therapy. Shortly after, she was also offered a position in a clinic, thereby quadrupling her income and allowing her to give up her clerical work.

Other people have reported the following improvements:

- An increase in counter sales
- An increase in client enquiries leading to increased work
- Wins from premium bonds or sweepstakes
- Sudden inspiration for a new line of work
- Inspiration for a different and more lucrative investment
- A bonus in the pay packet
- Unexpected gifts
- Unexpected opportunities for new ventures and profits
- Money from 'thin air'

This last point needs a little explanation and I would like to give an example by describing a small incident that happened to me.

We were on holiday in the South of France. My two children were eating endless ice creams and because of the expense I had been denying myself the pleasure of one of those scrumptious biscuit cones with three scoops of assorted flavours piled high with Chantilly cream. One day, however, I asked my dozing, or, more accurately as it turned out, my dozy, husband to keep the children well away from me while I sneaked off the beach for an assignation with the ice-cream stall.

Well, of course, he didn't. There I was, just about to take the first luscious bite out of my Chantilly when these little voices piped up: 'Can we have one?'

My husband didn't have quite enough change, so begrudgingly I paid for three more ices. It was my first year of using affirmations and I felt that either I had somehow sabotaged my Chantilly treat, or else the 'world out there' was still dealing me some mean tricks. As we walked back to the beach, I muttered to the family that the universe ought to pay me back for the thirty francs I had just paid out. Within seconds, my husband bent down and picked up two twenty-centime pieces (less than 1p) from the sandy pavement. He was laughing as he handed them to me and said, 'Looks like the universe doesn't think you're worth thirty francs.'

I took the coins from him and very seriously said aloud, 'I *do* deserve the full thirty francs,' at which my husband and children decided I had finally come off my trolley.

Not for long, though. Just a few yards along the road, my husband's foot scuffed against something that clinked in the sand. This time I was the one who bent down. There on the ground were three ten-franc coins.

The children were aghast. 'How ever did you do that? You just magicked it.'

Perhaps the coins had fallen from someone's pocket. Perhaps not. What I do know is that it was exactly the amount I thought I *deserved* and that is an excellent affirmation: 'I deserve an extra £ 000, (or a decent car, or new carpets, or whatever it happens to be). Exercises follow later that show you how to be specific with your own goals.

Don't stint yourself, especially if you're a woman and have been brought up with a 'serving' mentality. It's only by training your mind to believe in what might now seem impossible or extremely difficult that you will start to work 'miracles'.

My Own Experience and Success with these Processes

I first tried the goal-setting technique seven years ago in a workshop. I was very depressed at the time, feeling that my life was all slog and domestic chores (my two children were then very small). I seemed to be on a treadmill and the only money I could see coming in was the result of scrimping and self-denial.

Once I had written down my goals and divided them into the three sections described on p. 18, I had the overwhelming feeling that I needed extra money just to begin living a little. This was accompanied by an even more overwhelming feeling that achieving this was impossible. The workshop members encouraged me to say exactly what I needed to cover basic expenses and a few minor luxuries.

The figure I came up with was a capital sum that I wanted to invest to bring in an income. The amount, which ran into many thousands, shocked even them and left me feeling almost suicidal. It seemed so unobtainable and I felt condemned to go on merely existing. I had never been exposed to the workshop's ideas before, and was not to know then how brilliantly they work.

I spent the whole of the following weekend in a black pit of hopelessness, feeling that I was stuck in this rut for ever. In retrospect, I can see that this black pit consisted of my lack of self-esteem and all my negative ideas about money. What had actually happened was that I had opened the door on it and found myself looking at all the rubbish that had been holding me back my entire life.

A few days later, however, I suddenly had a gut feeling to place £1,000 in a particular investment. Within six months that £1,000 had brought me a £700 return and by the end of the year I had received a further £3,000 from sources I had never dreamt of.

Four years on, the sum of money I needed to begin living the life I had envisaged in my goals was achieved. In fact, I have since surpassed it and am now what the *Financial Times* calls 'moderately wealthy'.

Not one bit of it came from working. Most of it came from creative new ways of handling the money I already had (all of which are detailed in the following pages). I am still bowled over by the brilliance of the ideas and their success. The only thing that was necessary to start it all was to change my way of thinking.

Practical Steps to Make it Happen

Now that you have set your goals, short-term, medium-term and your wildest dream, and done a little mental 'clearing-out', it is time to get down to some practical work.

Do some spring-cleaning

You want your life to be a success. You want your finances to be profitable and to see results as fast as possible. You want everything to run as smoothly as a well-serviced machine so that you don't have to keep worrying. The first thing you must do, therefore, is remove all the accumulated debris and dirt from your life so that you can get things moving.

One of the simplest and most effective methods for giving your life a kick-start after a period of stagnation is to do some spring-cleaning.

It sounds simple, even trite, but clearing out your drawers and cupboards of all their accumulated debris and throwing it out, is like a physical affirmation. Your mind begins to see that you really are intent on clearing the decks for a fresh start to become more creative and receptive to the processes that follow.

Be quite ruthless. If you haven't used or worn something in the last two years, get rid of it. There might be the odd occasion later when you wish you had kept something, but the likelihood is that your life will have changed and you will have moved on. There are some items you will probably want to keep, such as jewellery or old treasures, so this is a good time to start wearing them or put them out on display.

The important thing is that from now on everything you own represents the person you are now, not some faded memory from a few years ago. Quite often we cling to certain ages in our life when we thought that life was especially good, wishing we could feel like we did when we were sixteen or twenty-five, or whatever. Our minds get stuck in a fantasy that has long since gone. No matter how difficult or good things may seem at present, this very hour, this very minute is where your future begins. This is when what you are thinking will create what happens to you later in the day or evening.

I am writing this at 7.30 in the morning, and writing it is like making an affirmation. Without doubt I shall be spending a creative day, stimulated into new ideas and ways of improving my finances, and spending a happy time with my family and friends.

Of course, some mornings I wake up and wish that I hadn't. The whole day seems to shuffle along as if it's all too much effort and I am wasting my time. This is a sure sign that there is rubbish in my psyche that needs chucking out. The simplest way to do this is to clear up something real like a pile of magazines and newspapers, or the fridge. It may not seem much at the time, but it will shift something and make room for a little progress.

Take control

Now that you have cleared up a bit, the real work

begins. It's time to change the way you look at your life.

Do you:

- Live from day to day, hoping for the best?
- Feel at the mercy of other people?
- Feel you have no control over larger financial issues, for example the bank rate or the ups and downs of the stock market?
- Have a fair idea of your plans, but are not sure that they will work out?

Well, none of this need be true. You can take control of your life to such a degree that you are at no one's mercy. Whatever misfortunes or successes occur in the outside world, your own life can remain secure.

You simply need to use your head. Your mind is a computer – the most sophisticated one in existence. All you have to do is programme it, let it do the work for you and keep a check that your programmes are up to date and designed to produce the results you want.

Set yourself a programme

This process is similar to the goal-setting exercise on p. 18 and can be used alongside it for comparison.

Now, however, we are going to be more focused, make sure that your time limits are specific and are not floundering in the realms of fantasy.

Take a new piece of paper and write at the top: *In five years, my ideal life will be . . .* Include money, home, relationships, work and travel. Let your imagination run free. Remember, this is not just about money, it is about prosperity, which covers all aspects of your life. When your list feels complete, compare it with the list you made setting out your wildest dreams (p. 18).

These two lists represent the ultimate, the things you want most of all. They contain your longings at their most unrestrained at this point in your life.

But are the lists different? Does your wildest dream look off the wall in comparison with your aims for five years' time? Does your five-year list look altogether more mundane, or do the lists tally very well?

The point is that they should tally, but you will probably find that your five-year list is fairly specific, whereas your 'wildest dream' may be vague.

Anything vague means that you have something to work on to bring it into reality.

For example, let us suppose your wildest dream is to be a millionaire and have several homes in various parts of the world, whilst your five-year list states that you want to be receiving £100,000 per annum. Start seeing that £100,000 as part of the million to come.

Play around with your goals. For example, if you achieved £1 million and had it invested at 10 per cent, it would be bringing you in £100,000. Furthermore, be sure to give yourself a pat on the back for every bit of extra money you receive, even for something as small as finding a 2p piece on the pavement. Several times, finding a 2p piece has been for me the precursor of something much larger.

If you find money, always pick it up no matter how silly you feel. I always say to myself that this is the beginning of something much bigger. OK, so you think I'm mad, but this was one of the ways I grew to be well off, and it can help you too.

Alternatively, let's suppose that in five years' time you want a large house with a swimming pool and jacuzzi. Start seeing that large house as a part of the million to come.

Your goals may be very different and not be concerned with such large sums of money, but the same rules apply: you must see each step as leading to the next and enjoy playing around with ideas as a child might. None of your dreams should be shunted into a never-never land of the 'It's impossible' variety. With a few exceptions, most very prosperous people achieved their goals step by step.

Make your dreams real

It is very important to bring your wildest dreams down to earth and make them 'real'.

Let's take the millionaire example again. If you are vaguely assuming that being a millionaire is better than your life now, try incorporating some of the qualities of that millionaire lifestyle into your own way of life. Make a list of the way you feel a millionaire lives. For example, you might think that he or she:

- Doesn't need to work
- Owns flashy cars
- Eats at expensive restaurants
- Wears expensive clothes
- Buys expensive presents
- Goes on exotic/luxurious holidays
- Pops over to Paris/Rome/Amsterdam/New York for a long weekend
- Has a big house or houses with indoor pool, jacuzzi and sauna

Then see what you can do right now to make some of these things a reality in your life.

For example, you could treat yourself to a meal in one of the best restaurants and tell yourself that you're doing it as part of the beginning of your new, prosperous future.

Perhaps your wildest dream is to laze around on a beach all day. First make a list of what this would entail:

- A house by the sea
- Money to cover living expenses
- Friends to alleviate boredom

Then do something practical like taking a fortnight off by the sea. Let your mind roam freely around the possibilities and you will probably come up with all sorts of new ideas for moving your life much more quickly into the directions you want it to go.

One friend who had such a dream decided to spend a fortnight in Spain and loved it so much she ended up putting a deposit on an apartment in the south. She was in her early thirties and had been a secretary in London. A long-term relationship had recently broken up so she decided to hand in her notice at work and spend a few months in her apartment.

She made new friends in Spain, and filled her spare time by painting local scenes of Andalucia to give herself some extra money for her modest lifestyle. Although she is not a great artist, her work is attractive and has opened up new areas of opportunity and given her a social life. Today she spends half the year back in London working as a temporary secretary and the rest of the time in her apartment in Spain.

Reviewing

This is essential.

Step 1   Every three months you must see how your short-term goals are progressing.

At first, progress may be slow or generally unexciting. *Don't give up.* This is the precise time when you should be persevering, when you should be revving up that sluggish motor.

Perhaps you have achieved only a small percentage of your goal, or perhaps you have exceeded your expectations. Whatever the result, after three months you must adjust your goals to incorporate your success.

For example, if your goal was an extra £500 at the end of three months and an extra £2,000 after twelve months, and within three months you receive £350, you only need another £1,650 to reach your target for twelve months. Write this down. This way you are acknowledging your success.

Step 2   Every six to nine months you need to overhaul your goals. They may be progressing well, but your life and motivations may have changed. Ask yourself:

- Am I happy with my life at the moment?
- If not, what would I like in my life?
- What do I need to do to bring this about?

Incorporate any new ideas arising from this into your goal-setting.

Step 3 Every twelve to eighteen months you need to rewrite your goals completely. You will have achieved some of them and moved far away from others.

You also need to check your five-year and wildest-dream lists. You are one to two years nearer these. How are they progressing? How does this make you feel?

Check that your five-year and wildest-dream lists are not different, if they are you are blocking yourself. You are saying to yourself that you can't have your wildest dream within three to four years. You are setting yourself up for it to remain a fantasy for a very long time.

In order to begin to correct this, transfer at least one important item from your wildest-dream list to your five-year list.

OK, so you're happily married and your wildest dream is to have a torrid affair with Tom Cruise.

Write this down.

It represents a deep, unfulfilled part of your psyche. Once you have acknowledged it and written it down, your computer brain can begin to work out the real problems and solutions, and at the right time a result will be produced.

Almost certainly it will not be Tom Cruise; maybe it won't even be an affair. Nevertheless, the result will be the perfect one for you.

Oh, so now you're disappointed. You're thinking, 'I can't have my wildest dream after all.'

Not so. Once you have actually made it clear in your mind what you really want, it often looks very different from your previous vague longing for exotic change. Once you have written it down and absorbed it, beneficial change will undoubtedly result.

Emma's story

Emma's wildest dream was to have umpteen affairs. She had been living with Kevin for three years. Her life was humdrum, with Kevin expecting his meals on the table promptly at fixed times. On Sundays he would stay in the pub until 3 pm and then come rolling back, half drunk, expecting his food. Afterwards he would slump in front of the TV for the rest of the day, swigging beer from the can.

It was not Emma's idea of happiness and certainly not how she wanted to spend the rest of her life.

So she went through these processes.

Her original 'If money and circumstance were no obstacle' list (see p. 7) stated: 'I would dump Kevin and find a new life.' Her five-year list mentioned a brilliant job that involved a lot of travelling. Her wildest-dream list mentioned the job plus several lovers who adored her.

She then began to write down her affirmations, such as:

- I, Emma, am now attracting the life I want
- I, Emma, can make my wildest dreams come true
- I, Emma, deserve to fulfil my wildest dreams
- Everything I want is flowing to me from an abundant universe

The result is that Emma now lives in a flat in London. Her job requires her to travel to Paris and New York periodically. To begin with she went wild and at one point had six different boyfriends on the go.

Emma was over the moon that she had achieved her 'fantasy', but after she had settled down she realised that what she really wanted was one permanent, loving mate. She therefore wrote affirmations for this (see Chapters 3 and 4). Shortly afterwards Chris arrived in her life and they are now happily married.

Emma is now the person she wanted to be a few years ago. She cleared her mind with the techniques I am giving you, and reprogrammed it with her goals and affirmations.

The only difference between Emma and you at this moment is belief. Emma knows that these processes work and is still using them to expand her life. When she sets her goals for three months ahead she doesn't know *how* the results will be achieved, but she does know that results are *bound to come* because she has done it before. As you begin to achieve results you will start to believe it too and the whole process will work much faster.

Speeding Up the Process

Here are some practical steps that will keep you going and speed things up.

Give something away

The idea behind this is to make a vacuum or channel for new things to flow to you. If you just hoard your money in a bank account, stagnations sets in.

Some people give money to a charity or buy a small gift for someone. Others give their time or take someone out for a treat. Because as a busy working mother I always seem to be giving to others, I usually turn the process round and instead buy myself something. It works a treat.

I make a definite commitment to buy this 'gift' for myself and I turn the whole thing into an affirmation of my desire for prosperity: the trip into town to buy it, perhaps a nice lunch with a friend, the purchase itself.

This is an important point. You must always honour yourself. Never allow anyone to persuade you into believing that someone else is more important than you are. They may be *as* important, but not *more*. Never underestimate your own value. You are the centre of your universe and you deserve the best that you can give yourself. The only thing you truly possess is your body and your mind, so look after and pamper them.

Use the 'law of ten'

The law of ten comes from the Bible. The desert tribes used to reserve a tenth of their harvest to use as seed for the following year, and this technique is a variation of that idea.

Say, for example, that you want to attract an extra £1,000 into your life. See if you already possess £100, that is 10 per cent of your target sum, and look at this as the seeds of your £1,000. If you are strapped for cash, then start with 10 per cent of £100, and use this, and if you really don't have £10 start with just £1.

Now, you either save your 10 per cent 'seed' in an interest-bearing account and say to yourself that this will grow into £1,000, or you spend *some* of it on a treat with the express purpose of attracting other good things into your life.

It is important not to be completely reckless at this stage. If you are really short of cash and need £100 for bills, don't scare yourself by blowing the lot on this exercise. Use 10 per cent of what you have until you build up confidence in your ability to create prosperity and have what is known as 'prosperity consciousness'.

But don't stop once you have invested your 10 per cent. If you have bought an item, you must use it consciously, knowing that it is your seed. If you have saved the money, every time interest is paid you must withdraw between 10 and 50 per cent and spend it, affirming to yourself that you are already attracting the £1,000 you are aiming at. If you have only saved £1, you'll have to use your imagination and maybe do some affirmative window-shopping. The point is that you are enjoying your money while it is still growing, and I can guarantee that it will grow faster than any arithmetical calculations say it will because your mind starts to become much more creative.

What you are in fact doing is making a very positive statement about your life and what you want in it, and this has a magnetic effect. You start to feel better, whether or not you fully believe in the process, and the magnetism set up by these good feelings starts to create results and results create belief. Once that belief is there, the shape of the third phalange of your finger will begin to change.

Prosperity lunches/suppers/dinners

If you can enlist the support of a friend to help you with these ideas it will improve your progress dramatically. It's an excellent way of combining a social occasion with increasing your prosperity. All that is necessary is for you to set your targets for the next three months and discuss your achievements. Since three months is the shortest goal-setting time, it is a good idea to arrange quarterly meetings.

I have two principal 'prosperity friends' whom I meet separately at least once a quarter. We always meet for a meal, when we set and write down our targets. We also review our progress and achievements since our last meeting. We talk about how our lives seem to be going and bounce ideas for improvement off one another. Of course, it's not all serious stuff. The important thing is to enjoy it and have fun.

At first you may feel silly about including a friend in your goal-setting and that's absolutely fine. When you start to achieve results you'll find you can't help telling people about it and as your enthusiasm helps other people to succeed, you will find that this gives you an extra boost. But do be sure that the people in whom you confide your goals fully support you. Jealousy and envy can sometimes creep in and anyone like this should be avoided.

Surround yourself with positive people

This is a time when you will begin to notice more than ever those people who are positive and enhance your life and your aspirations and those who pull you down.

Life is magnetic. Like attracts like. If you are around

negative people you will attract those energies to yourself. If you are around positive people, you will attract
better things.

For example, a rich banker's wife invited a friend of
mine to lunch at an expensive restaurant in London. My
friend's goals had been hovering around a short-term
£3,000.

The banker's wife was very interested in these ideas
and gently probed to discover her goals. When she told
her, she smiled broadly and asked, 'Why are you setting
your sights so low? Why aren't you going for an extra
£30,000?'

My friend experienced a sudden surge of despair. How
could she bring in £30,000 in three months? Despite her
firm beliefs in creating prosperity, it seemed beyond her
current abilities. She hadn't imagined herself with that
sort of money to play with. At that rate she could be
moving towards £120,000 a year in addition to her current
income.

Her reply was that she couldn't cope with aiming for
such a large sum, she didn't feel 'magnetic' enough to
attract that kind of money, but she would go for an extra
£10,000, even though that seemed pretty impossible.
She simply couldn't see how she could become that
creative.

Even as she was saying this, almost immediately behind
the despair came exhilaration. She knew that she was
being lifted up to another level.

The result was that she did make an extra £6,000 in
those three months. Not quite the £10,000 she was aiming
for because of her doubts and limitations, but still double
what she had originally set herself – and all of it came
from new creative ideas.

The banker's wife had lived a life of luxury and
opulence, while my friend had lived one full of struggles
and difficulty. She would never have opened the doors in
her mind to expand her ideas if she hadn't been 'touched'
by the other woman's magnetism and belief. Above all,
the experience was great fun!

Immersing yourself in prosperity and opulence

As in the story of my friend's lunch with the banker's wife, you can absorb prosperity by having coffee or tea at the best hotels and restaurants, even lunch or dinner if you really want to push the boat out. If you go by yourself, take note of the people around you, absorb some of their self-assurance around money.

Go to the most expensive boutiques and shops and look at the clothes. Imagine yourself wearing them and even try them on. Once you start getting results, treat yourself to something expensive.

Go and look at the best that life has to offer and believe that you can have it.

Attracting your goals

To further reinforce the energy and magnetism, it is a good idea to do some small thing towards it, to create a 'yeast' to make it grow, to make a small magnet and channel to draw it towards you.

Let's suppose that your goal is a new home but you currently lack the money for a deposit. Buy something small for the house you want. If the rooms are going to be larger, buy something new to go in them, perhaps a small table or an ornament, and say to yourself that this is for your new home.

If you want a new car, buy the manuals for it and peruse them, telling yourself that this is in preparation for actually having it. One man I know wanted an MG sports car so badly that he bought seat covers for it, as well as spray paint in his favourite colour and a car vacuum for cleaning it.

Today he has his MG. It was blue and rusty when he bought it, but it's now the sunflower yellow he wanted. He says he feels like a millionaire in it and has noticed improvements in all areas of his life since he has had it.

Perhaps you simply want a lot more money to give you the freedom to pursue your larger goals. What will your lifestyle be like with this money? More luxurious obviously, so start now with more affordable comforts. Some smoked salmon perhaps? Half a bottle of champagne? Upmarket shirts and ties? A designer scarf?

Purchase these things consciously, saying to yourself that this is the beginning of your new lifestyle, the channel by which your goals can begin to be realized.

Buy yourself a 'prosperity' mug

Buy yourself a mug for your coffee or tea which has a design on it that sums up your goals.

One friend bought one with a basketful of harvest fruits and vegetables. She felt that her goals were epitomised by the idea of harvest and completion. Another friend bought one with balloons on it because they symbolised her creative ideas floating up into the air and reaching far off places. Another bought one patterned in rich colours and goldleaf because it looked so gorgeous and opulent.

Each time you drink from it, the mug will subliminally remind you of your goals, and because the drink itself is refreshing you, you will feel that you are actually absorbing this affirmation of your aims. It is one of the most intimate affirmations you can make.

Pay yourself

This is another approach to the law of ten. If you can manage it, pay yourself 10 per cent of your income or, at the very least, 10 per cent of what you have left over from your pay, and invest it. The idea is for this to grow and make you financially independent.

It is an interesting fact that many Americans are totally comfortable with the idea of financial independence, i.e. not needing to work for a living, while in Great Britain only a very small percentage of us are. Those who are tend to be the clear thinkers who have made it.

I have lost count of the number of people who have responded to the idea of this sort of prosperity with, 'It seems wrong to get money without working hard for it.'

Who says so? Why is it wrong? Isn't it worse to be working all day every day in a job that doesn't fulfil you and pays you a pittance? Of course, if it's a job that you love, it won't feel like hard work anyway, but you should be living comfortably, not struggling.

It is also a fact, pointed out by Mark Haroldsen in his book *How to Wake Up the Financial Genius Inside You*, that if you invest £10,000 at an interest rate of 25 per cent and reinvest the interest, in twenty-one years you will have more than £1 million.

Furthermore, 25 per cent is not so difficult to achieve, as you will discover once you really start to buzz with the success of your results and amazing new opportunities begin to open up.

The key is *joy*. Money is energy and as your own energy rises with the pleasure of trying these techniques and sharing them with supportive friends, success in some measure or form is absolutely assured. It just flows to you. If you start feeling low and negative, everything begins to slow down. Your prosperity engine clogs up.

A friend decided to prove the point and opened a 10 per cent prosperity account in a building society. At first she just put in the surplus from her salary after all bills and needs were accounted for. This amounted to £5 per week. She started doing this in November, which meant that by the following March she should have had around £100. In fact she had nearer £800. She insists that she doesn't know exactly how this happened, except that for the first time in years she seemed to have more than £5 surplus every week, and that just after Christmas she hit on a brilliant idea to make some extra pocket money. Even that, however, did not fully account for the increase. All she knew was that she felt buoyant and prosperous and it just seemed to happen. In fact, it was the buoyancy that did it: it made her creative with the way she used her money.

Prosperity bank accounts

This is an extension of paying yourself. We are all familiar with the idea of savings accounts, which usually conjure up an image of painstaking, piecemeal offerings to the bank, building society or post office. By their very nature they make us feel that acquiring money is a hard, gradual slog, and thus tend to reinforce the idea that real wealth is not for us. For this reason we need to wake ourselves up and open some fun accounts.

The financial independence account How much money do you need to become financially independent? By that I mean how much money do you need to stop working for a living for ever? Is it £100,000 invested at 10 per cent, bringing in a net income of £10,000 a year? Is it £200,000 or even £500,000?

Come on, really think about it. Not thinking about it seriously and not believing it is possible is what keeps millions of us slogging away for a pittance all our lives.

Let's forget about pensions, winnings and hand-outs for a minute. Let's only think about the fun of making it for ourselves and being able to work only when we want to long before retirement age.

I have to admit that by using all the techniques in this chapter, I am already getting close to this enviable position. Playing around with building-society accounts was just one of the many fun ways I did it.

Admittedly, I opened my 'financial independence' account with the Halifax Building Society when interest rates were high, but that really doesn't make very much difference because we're working on lifting the mind from its linear, one-track mode. Into this account I put whatever I had over in change each week. Sometimes it was £5, more often only £2 or £3. Because the interest was payable half-yearly, twice a year I would go and draw out *half* the interest and use it as I imagined I would if I were financially independent.

At the end of the first six months the interest was the princely sum of £4.20, but I was determined to use £2.10 of this as if I were financially independent and free from worries about money, so I spent the morning browsing around expensive shops, imagining myself buying lovely things. I used 70p on a cup of coffee and the remaining £1.40 on an afternoon swim and sauna. I cheated a bit and added something to pay for lunch and the sauna, but the important thing was that it hugely expanded my sense of wellbeing and my awareness of new possibilities.

The next interest payment was £16 partly due to the fact that I had managed to make larger deposits during the second six months. I think this was because my ideas for creating prosperity were beginning to expand. I took out £8, which enabled me to spend a much more satisfying day. A year later I was able to extend the time to two days and spend the money on more luxurious things.

The whole purpose of using such an account is to give you a real affirmation of what financial independence might be like for you.

Normally when we give ourselves treats such as a good meal or a visit to the theatre we are thinking in terms of taking money from our accounts. This creates a sense of loss, of maybe having to forego something else in order to do this.

With this account you are free to spend the interest knowing that the money is growing and will give you larger and larger amounts each half-year until real financial independence becomes a possibility.

Once I started working with these techniques, my resistance to wealth rapidly fell away, and, in proportion to that lowering of resistance, my prosperity grew. Within three years of working with these techniques I was able to take six weeks off in addition to normal holidays, and I found that the more time I gave myself, the more prosperous I became. The following affirmation became true for me: 'The more time I give myself and the less I waste time on things I don't love, the more money I have and the more my deepest dreams are coming into reality.'

As a small postscript here, while interest rates are low I suggest you take out most of the interest and just leave a token 10p or 50p, otherwise you may get thrust back into the idea that financial independence takes an awful long time to achieve. In addition, many building societies now only pay out interest yearly, so scout around for accounts that pay out more often.

One trick I used was to close the account every half-year and reopen it within the week. That way they were obliged to pay me whatever interest had accrued. If you feel silly doing that in the same building society, simply close it in one society after six months and open up somewhere else. It's your money and the building societies are making more money out of you than you are out of them, so use them to build your own fortune.

The millionaire's account This sounded quite preposterous to my husband when I opened it one Christmas at the Abbey National. I wrote on a small piece of paper that this was my millionaire's account and inserted it in my passbook so that I would read it every time I made a deposit.

My husband soon changed his tune when he saw how rapidly it grew. I used it in conjunction with my financial independence account, dividing up my spare cash between them. Each time I went through the sliding doors of the Abbey National I would say to myself: 'I'm putting a deposit in my millionaire's account.'

I know it sounds loony, but who else is going to tell me that I have the opportunity to be a millionaire? No one else cares, and it is a huge affirmation.

Until seven years ago I had never thought in terms of anything other than simply getting by and saving up for good holidays and clothes. Since working with these techniques, however, I've discovered how rapidly money flows when there are no mental obstacles. Our subconscious minds cannot distinguish between what is real and what is imaginary. Our bodies will respond to a horror film by producing adrenaline just as if we believed the danger was real. Give your mind imaginary wealth and it will start to produce new ideas and opportunities.

With the millionaire's account you spend half the interest on luxury items. At the beginning it is hard to find a mega-luxury item for £2 or so, but I found a bistro selling superb mocha coffees piled high with cream for £1.30, whilst a friend blew her first millionaire's interest payment on a tequila sunrise in a cocktail lounge where she was propositioned by a wealthy businessman.

Of course, he was married and she told him to shove off, but it opened her eyes to the idea that if you want a millionaire, you have to go where the millionaires go. It also made her realise that she would rather make her own million than try to find some wealthy man to support her. Either way, her ideas about money received an important boost.

The Last Word

You are the most important person in your life, but have you been limiting yourself financially? Your life is not a dress rehearsal. This is it, so decide what you want and *go for it.*

3

Take Control of Your Love Life

'The English don't have lovers; they have hot-water
bottles'

French saying

Just how vital physical affection is to us was demonstrated in studies made some years ago on monkeys. One
group of newborns were separated from their mothers and
placed in individual cages where they were given all the
nourishment they needed in feeder trays but could not
see each other. In other words, they lacked the sensory
stimulation of the touch, sight, smell and sound of their
own kind. These monkeys failed to flourish. When
compared with a group of controls who had been left
with their mothers, they were underweight, undersized,
and their immune systems were impaired, making them
vulnerable to disease.

Human beings are the same.

Unlike the pursuit of prosperity, which needs only your
mind and your brain, your love life is rooted in your
emotions and involves another human being. Success in
this field, therefore, requires a different approach.

The lines on the palm of your hand tell the story not
only of your emotional experience in the past, but also
of what is to come. If you don't like the look of the
patterns that appear there, you can begin to change
them. If you can see that you are heading for a series
of bad love affairs, you can avoid trouble and start
attracting what you want. It is also a good idea to

consider why difficult patterns are appearing there in the first place.

What thoughts do you have that are setting you up for difficult experiences? Are they to do with low self-esteem? For example, do you think:

'I'm not good-looking enough to hold on to him/her.'

'I never seem to attract the right type.'

'Love scares me. It's all so hit and miss.'

Or do you expect too much? Do you find yourself thinking:

'I wouldn't touch him or her with a barge pole.'

'I'm not going out with someone who looks like that.'

'If he/she hasn't got a good bank balance they can forget it.'

Whatever your position, you can improve it.

The areas of the hands that show the emotional life are the cusp of the palm just below the little finger and the long affection lines that travel across the mount of Venus (the fleshy pad at the base of the thumb), across the lifeline, the head line and the heart line, and end

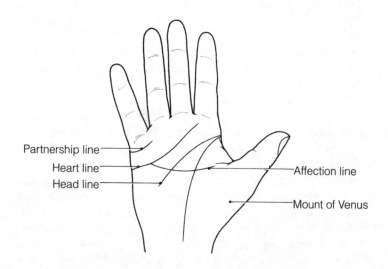

up on the mount of Mercury (the pad below the little finger), close to the cusp with the other love lines (fig. 3.1). Partnership lines are found on the cusp of the mount of Mercury and will be dealt with in Chapter 4.

Affection lines can often be faint, and are not usually as strong as the major lines of life, head and heart, though more important relationships such as a long-term lover or partner will show up in stronger lines. Otherwise, it is quite common for single people to have a mass of faint lines going across the palm. The more romantic you are, the more likely you are to have these patterns.

The length of the affection lines and the important lines they cross are indicative of the central part played by love relationships in our lives. The way they cross the lines of life, head and heart shows how they affect the sum total of who we are. We cannot manipulate them in the same way we can the lines and patterns indicating health, longevity and prosperity, largely because they concern another human being. While we can work on ourselves and create enormous developments in our favour, we cannot work on someone else. Of course we can try, but it usually results in failure and the object of our affections running for the nearest exit.

What we can do, however, is to become clear in our minds what we are looking for in a mate or lover and start to remove the blocks within ourselves that are hindering us. In this chapter I am first of all going to explain the predictive indicators on the hand – those lines that mean a good love affair and those that mean a poor one; as well as what to do if you have a poor line, or if you are so besotted that you refuse to give up.

Finally, we shall look at ways to attract the 'perfect' someone and create a completely new line altogether. I have put the word 'perfect' in inverted commas because some people have managed to attract some pretty bizarre Mr/Ms Perfects through omitting some vital detail in their blueprints and visualisations. But more of that later.

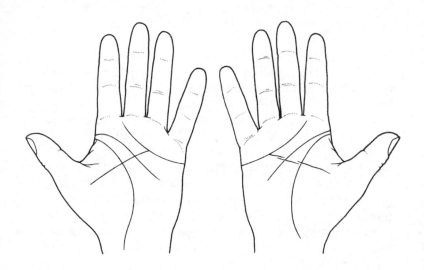

Reading Your Hands

You will remember from Chapter 1 that the left hand is
the 'hand of destiny' and represents the patterns imprinted
at birth; in folk culture, it is regarded as the true hand. The
right hand represents what we make of our lives and is
therefore much more a creation of our conscious minds.
Now look at the diagrams in figure 3.2, which show some
typical affection-line configurations, and compare them
with your own patterns.

In figure 3.2a, the strong line on the left hand means that
a good relationship is due and has a good chance of success. However, the wavy line on the right hand means that
you are not very confident of it. This doubt and lack of
confidence may be the result of a previous experience, or
perhaps the loved one isn't living up to your expectations.

In this situation, it is a good idea to look again at
the relationship. If it is only self-doubt or anxiety

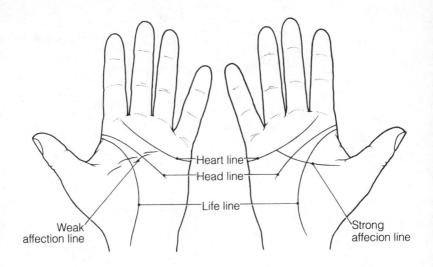

that is holding things back, in every other respect the relationship has the right foundations for success. In addition, this pattern of lines means you are in the driving seat. You are the one deciding for or against the affair. You may not think so if you are feeling upset by the actions of your beloved or your confidence is low, but the strength of the line on your left hand clearly states that the bond between you can be a good one if the factors revealed by the weak right line can be overlooked or overcome.

With 3.2(b) the position is reversed. In this case, the weakness of the line on the left hand means that this love affair was meant to come into your life but it was not meant to be an easy or even happy experience. It would be better to love and leave, move on and forget. The strength of the line on the right hand, however, means that you have fallen hopelessly in love and are refusing to accept all the warning signals.

Of all the affection line configurations, this is the most difficult, but the situation is not impossible. One of my

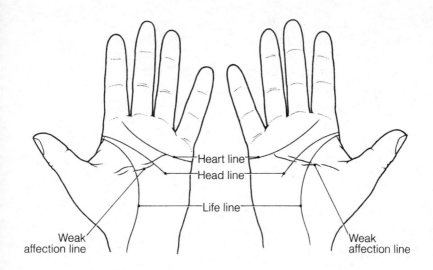

oldest friends had this pattern on her own hands when she met her husband. Just before they were married a group of us went down to Brighton for the day, and on an impulse my friend popped into the fortune-teller's tent on the pier. As the gypsy pulled the curtain, she glanced outside at my friend's fiancé. We all heard her say, 'Don't you go marrying that man out there, he'll bring you a hard life.' Of course, my friend suspected that already, but wasn't prepared to listen. Not many people are when their emotions are in control.

Well, her overpowering right-hand line won the day.

She did marry and the fortune-teller was right. They went through hell for the first few years with all the external problems of money and family. Eventually, however, they came out on the other side. My friend's weak left-hand affection line developed a loop to emerge higher up the lifeline to the point where things began to get better and a new line developed. In fact, the new line looks almost like a new relationship, which is in fact what their marriage became.

So, if you have this configuration of a feathery left-hand line and a strong right-hand one and decide to battle against the odds, you may still succeed.

Figure 3.2(c) shows a person with weak lines on both hands. This means that the relationship wasn't meant to be ideal but you've got your eyes open and are seeing it for what it is. As with (b) above, if you are looking for happiness and ease it would be better to let this love affair go. However, quite often when people with these lines marry, they are setting themselves up for a great deal of difficulty unless they get clear on why they entered the relationship in the first place. If they do this, though, and stick with the relationship, sometimes the most extraordinary transformations can take place – rather like turning base metal into gold.

Figure 3.2(d) shows the ideal position. Both lines are strong, which means that the relationship is meant to be a good one and that you are fulfilled by it.

One question I am always asked is about timing – when is it going to happen?

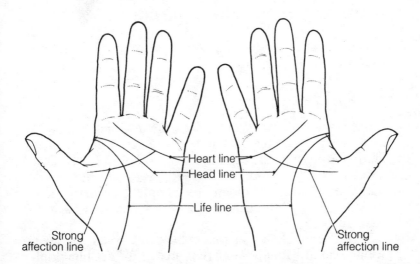

It is difficult to give an exact rule for everyone as hands vary so much in shape and size. As a rough guide, on the lifeline a centimetre represents approximately ten years, starting between the thumb and the index finger. If your hand is very small you need to reduce this to say 8–9 mm; if very large, increase it slightly. You can work out approximately how many millimetres represent ten years on your own hands by checking your lines for those relationships that have already occurred, but if there are no lines until quite late, or if you are very young, just use the rough guide above to give you an approximate idea of when any love affairs will occur in your life. Some people's hands show lines very early on in their life, say at about seven or eight. Although these can indicate a crush on someone, they can also mean a beloved pet or a close bond with a parent or caring adult.

So now you have checked the lines on your hands. No matter what kind of lines you have, whether they seem wavy or nonexistent, and whether you want to attract a new relationship or sort out an existing one that isn't working, you can begin to make it happen.

Attracting a New Relationship

The techniques below will show you how to bring the right love into your life.

Make a blueprint

Take a piece of paper and list all the qualities you want in a lover or partner. Include character traits such as kind, fun-loving, etc, but also state quite clearly how you would like him or her to look. Beauty is in the eye of the beholder, so simply putting 'good-looking' will still clear the way for the love that is right for you.

It is essential that you are very specific about what you want. One girl found the perfect match for her blueprint:

tall, dark and handsome, with a good income, a nice car and an apartment. However, he was also bisexual, running her alongside his male lover.

Another man made a similar mistake. He said that he wanted a beautiful blonde and an apartment in the capital. He meant London but didn't say so. Well, he got his blonde, but she is Dutch and the apartment is in Amsterdam. Of course, there's absolutely nothing wrong with that. He's probably better off in Amsterdam, but it is better to be aware of how specific you need to be. (Incidentally, once he had made the move to Holland, it showed on his hand that he had left England for Europe.)

Now that you have your blueprint, put it somewhere safe and forget about it while you get on with sorting yourself out. The blueprint has entered your subconscious mind and will be helping you towards achieving your goals.

Feel good about yourself

Step 1 Take another piece of paper and list all the reasons why you think your love life is not the way you want it to be. List all those negative feelings you have about yourself, such as:

1. I can't seem to find suitable/eligible women/men
2. Men think I am supercapable but unfeminine
3. Women think I'm a wimp
4. Men like kittenish women
5. Women seem to like the strong, hunky type
6. All the decent men/women already have partners
7. I'm too fat
8. I'm too thin
9. I'm embarrassed for anyone to see me naked
10. I'm not very good in bed
11. I'm brilliant in bed but my partner's not so hot
12. I can't reach orgasm
13. I come too quickly
14. My thighs are enormous

15. You need a search party to find my breasts
16. Men only want sex
17. Women only want romance
18. Men are selfish bastards
19. Women are demanding
20. I'm past it. Potential lovers are going to want a younger, racier version

Include even the most apparently insignificant things because each comment represents a thought that has helped to create those feathery lines on your hands. Change those thoughts and your affection lines are *bound* to improve. You won't necessarily land the gorgeous blonde at the office or the muscled hunk at the squash club, but you will certainly begin to change your feelings about yourself, and other people will pick that up. You will automatically start to become more confident, attractive, magnetic.

Step 2 So let's suppose that your list is similar to the one above. All you do is change it around so that your mind is programmed to accept a different image of yourself. For example, you could change the points in the above list as follows (don't forget to insert your first name):

1. I—am now coming across eligible men/women wherever I go
2. Men admire me exactly as I am
3. Women are attracted to me exactly as I am
4. Men like my style and looks
5. Women like my looks and personality
6. There are plenty of available, gorgeous, eligible men/women
7. I—am exactly the right size for me. Any excess weight now drops off easily, and I look good whatever size I am
8. My body is the right shape for my bone structure. People see me as attractive
9. I—am completely happy with my body and sexuality

10. I—am getting better and better in bed
11. I—am brilliant in bed and I'm learning to be patient with my partner
12. Maybe I—haven't reached orgasm yet, but practise makes perfect
13. I—am learning to slow down and satisfy myself and my partner completely
14. My thighs are perfect and sexy
15. Small is beautiful: my breasts are the perfect size for my beautiful body
16. I—now enjoy what men want and they enjoy everything I am
17. I—am now beginning to understand women more, so that we both have a good time
18. I—now release my negative feelings about men. I no longer let past experiences upset my future. *Or*: Men are gorgeous, exciting, fun, as well as sometimes being selfish bastards
19. My life is now changing for the better. As it does so, I attract only lovely people to me. *Or*: Women are delicious, desirable, sensitive and sometimes demanding
20. Every age is wonderful. I—am the ideal person for the lover/partner I am now attracting to me. *Or*: I—am mature, desirable and racy enough for anyone

The whole point is that feeling negative and rotten about yourself and other people is only a state of mind, not necessarily the truth. But a depressive state of mind is unattractive and you will repel people. As a result your negative thoughts begin to become a reality.

The reverse is also true. Begin to feel positive and happy, even if only slightly, and you will create a different electrical charge around yourself that will be a magnet to others.

Your mind is all-powerful. It can create absolutely everything you want. It can even change your shape (see Chapter 5). Once you begin to remove all those niggling doubts about your looks, your personality and your sexuality, the real, vibrant you can begin to emerge and attract the love(s) you want. Here are some more affirmations you can make to yourself. Don't forget to personalise them by inserting your first name after the 'I'.

- I—am gorgeous, desirable and sexy
- I—am becoming more desirable and lovable every day that passes
- I—deserve a wonderful mate/lover
- I—am attracting right now a lover/mate who adores me
- I—am attracting right now the perfect partner for me

Dealing with Difficult Relationships

When a relationship finishes for whatever reason, the chances are that you will not come out of it unscathed. If you are not the one who calls it a day, it will dent your self-esteem badly, and this will be more or less obvious to those around you. You will start to feel that there is something wrong with you, that you're not attractive or sexy enough, and, most damaging of all, that perhaps you're not the type who will ever hold on to a relationship. As a result, when you do meet someone else, these doubts and fears will create their own problems, or you may opt for safety and choose someone less attractive or with a less exciting lifestyle than you would like because you feel you can hold on to him or her. It's important, therefore, to know when a relationship is not working for you and to be able to deal with this in a positive, self-enhancing way. The following stories show how it is possible to achieve this.

Vicky's story

Vicky is a very beautiful woman who has naturally

attracted a lot of male attention. All through her teens she was aware of the power of her looks and used it to the full by having a good time with all the most attractive men available. She had been brought up in the country where the pace of life is slow and the men, by and large, honest and above board. When she moved to London and became a model, the men she attracted were of a different type altogether: happy to have her on their arms, looking good; happy to treat her to the high life, but not interested in anything serious.

She fell deeply, hopelessly in love with one such man, who, after a few months, dumped her. She couldn't believe it. It had never happened to her before. She was sure it had to be an aberration, a one-off. So, still with a strong self-image of her own beauty, she attracted and fell in love again with another man just like the first. He, too, dumped her.

Things deteriorated rapidly. She got through seven love affairs in a fairly short space of time and each time her self-esteem plummeted, so that by the time I met her, Vicky's beauty was hollow. She felt worthless, unattractive and as if it was all her fault.

Both of Vicky's hands showed a series of feathery lines representing the series of bad love affairs. However, a strong affection line on her left hand and a weak one on her right (see figure 3.2(a), p. 48) revealed that a new pattern was about to develop in her life, which is exactly what happened.

He was a gentle, home-loving man, quite good-looking, but not one of the Adonis types she had previously fallen for, and quite comfortably off, though not with the megabucks she had become accustomed to. All her feelings of worthlessness surfaced.

Deep down she didn't think that this man was good enough for her, hence the feathery line on her right hand. He wasn't what she was used to. For the first time in her life she felt that she couldn't have what she wanted and that in accepting him she was taking second best.

But the strength of the left-hand line carried the day.

The man truly loved her, especially her damaged psyche, which made her vulnerable. In her former, high-flying days he would have been scared even to approach her. Eventually she grew to love him too and today they are happily married.

Vicky is still very beautiful, even more so because she is fulfilled, and thanks to the support of her husband she has started a business that makes use of many of her old high-flying contacts, including some of her ex-lovers. She found happiness by using the following techniques.

First of all, she wrote a list of all the reasons she thought things had gone wrong. For example:

1. I am always falling in love with men who don't love me
2. I am always attracting the wrong type
3. I can't hold on to gorgeous men

She then turned all her negatives into positive affirmations:

1. I now fall in love with men who love me
2. I am now attracting sincere and lovely men
3. I am now able to hold on to gorgeous men

She then made her blueprint, stating the qualities she wanted in her perfect mate. Because of all her failures with extremely rich, desirable men, she concentrated on qualities such as being kind, loving, sincere and supportive.

Finally, she sat down for at least ten minutes a day to visualise her life as she wanted to live it. By now she was tired of the high life and was ready to settle down, so she saw herself in more domestic surroundings with a nice house, the partner of her dreams and the lifestyle she wanted.

Of course, what is obvious from her story is that she had always placed too much value on her own looks and those of the men in whom she was interested. Her love destiny, as revealed in her hands, had been to suffer several faulty relationships until she came to understand that there was more to herself and others than glitter and gloss.

If Vicky had started work on herself earlier, she would have erased most of those feathery lines in her right and left hands representing the poor love affairs and achieved happiness sooner. Quite often, however, where love is concerned we don't want to see what is obvious to others. We want to hang on to our illusions. Even when our eyes are opened, it takes time to change the emotional patterns that have built up since childhood. As a result, affection lines can sometimes take quite a bit longer than prosperity ones to develop satisfactory patterns.

Eleanor's story

Eleanor had this pattern on her hands: a weak, feathery line on her left hand and a strong line on her right (see figure 3.2(b), p. 49). She was an extremely pretty woman in her late forties who had just emerged from a long but unhappy marriage.

It was Eleanor who had decided to leave the marriage and consequently she felt strong and purposeful. She worked for a garage selling up-market cars like BMW and Mercedes and was flattered to receive a lot of attention from male purchasers.

There was no shortage of admirers but the affair revealed in the pattern on her palm turned out to involve a man in his early thirties who loved Eleanor for her beauty, her fun and her homemaking qualities. However, as the strong line on Eleanor's right hand showed; she refused to see that this relationship didn't have a strong foundation. Instead, she plunged in blindly, giving him all she had.

From her marriage, Eleanor had come away with half the proceeds from the marital home, and these she pooled with her younger lover. They lived together for some time before she discovered that his 'business meetings' were trysts with nubile girls. In other words, he was happy to have Eleanor at home looking after all his needs as long as he also continued to have the freedom of a single man.

How Eleanor escaped

Like Vicky, Eleanor was able to escape from her unhappy situation by using the techniques I have outlined. First of all she listed the reasons she thought had landed her in this mess. The main one was the sudden sense of freedom she had experienced after her marriage was over, and her belief that she could have any man she wanted. Although these could have been positive qualities, they had blinded her to reality. Now, therefore, she needed to build up her self-esteem with affirmations like:

- I, Eleanor, am a beautiful, desirable woman
- I, Eleanor, am now attracting the perfect partner for me
- I, Eleanor, am now attracting a man who will love and cherish me

Eleanor's money

Money was also a major problem because it was tied up in the house she had bought with her younger lover. She therefore had to begin some serious affirmative and visualisation work on her finances and prosperity.

Within a matter of weeks, she had found another job paying her half as much again as the garage, plus commission. This enabled her to move into a flat while the house was put on the market. Of course, the lover was up in arms, telling her that he loved her and that she was the only one for him.

Silly Eleanor gave him another chance, taking the house off the market and moving back in. Within weeks, of course, she discovered that not only was he still seeing his 'girls' but that he was buying them presents with Eleanor's petty cash.

That was the end of it. The lover finally got the boot. Eleanor got her share of the house and is now the successful manageress of another business with a warm, dependable new partner.

Reinforcing Your Progress

Whatever problem you are dealing with, it's important that you continue the good work you have begun with the above techniques by reinforcing your affirmations.

Make a tape

There are some excellent self-help tapes on the market from specialist bookshops (see Appendix), but in order to have something uniquely your own, and therefore much more effective, you can make one yourself.

There are two sorts: one repeats affirmations in a straightforward way, the other works subliminally.

To make the first kind, start by writing down the affirmations that have emerged from your list in step 1 (see p. 53), adding any others that appeal to you. Some good general affirmations (don't forget to insert your first name after 'I') are:

1. I—can have what I want
2. I—don't have to settle for second best
3. Everyone has value and we can all have fun
4. I—attract fun and friendship wherever I am
5. Life is for living and wonderful new opportunities are appearing in my life right now
6. New friends and potential lovers are being attracted into my life right now
7. I—am lovable and desirable
8. New friends are deeply attracted to me
9. I—now allow the best in me to emerge
10. All the people in my life now see the best in me
11. I—release all doubts about my desirability
12. I—am lovable, desirable and sexy
13. I—no longer feel separate and distant
14. I can now allow all my old barriers to intimacy to come down

15. I—now feel that I am as attractive as anyone else
16. I enjoy being me more and more every day
17. I now realise that I really like me
18. I—am actually pretty darned marvellous and I feel good in my body
19. I—love using my body to express myself
20. I—no longer shrink inside my body
21. The more I enjoy my body, the more gorgeous it becomes and the more other people are attracted to me
22. My perfect lover/partner is being attracted into my life right now

You can make the list as long or short as you like, but as you write it is a good exercise just to let your mind roam free so that some of your wildest fantasies can emerge. If images of steamy orgies and having absolutely anything and anyone any way you want fill your mind, then write them down.

If you get stuck and your mind goes blank, try to think of scenes where you are the life and soul of the party, where potential friends or lovers are clamouring to talk or to dance with you, or to date you. If parties don't appeal, think of a scenario that shows you at some peak of popularity – perhaps at work or on holiday. Once you've got the picture in your mind, write down the appropriate affirmations, for example:

- Wonderful social opportunities now arise where I can meet lovely new people/friends/lovers
- I am never at a loss for words
- I am popular
- I am gorgeous and desirable
- Everyone I meet is fascinated by me
- My body is daily more gorgeous and desirable
- Everyone I meet admires me
- I find something likeable in everyone I meet
- The more I find others attractive, the more attractive they find me

- All my barriers to love are now coming down
- I am open and free and happy
- Others are open, free and happy with me
- The world is my oyster: the more I fulfil my true self the more others are fulfilled by me

Actually making the tape

When you feel that your list is as complete as you can make it, you are ready to record it on a cassette. If you have two machines or a radio you can, if you like, play some background music at the same time as you are recording your affirmations to make them more effective. You don't have to fill the whole tape, although it does save continually having to rewind it to listen if you do.

Alternatively, if you have a machine with a double tape deck or can use a friend's, you can save yourself an hour or so of talking. To do this, record your chosen list of affirmations on one tape, say about five minutes of recording. Then rewind what you have done and record it on to a fresh tape in the second deck.

When your five minutes or so of affirmations on the first tape come to an end, stop both tapes, rewind the first and start recording it on to the second tape again. Repeat this process until the second tape is filled or until you've had enough. Although you have to keep fiddling with the rewind and record buttons, it does save your voice – unless you feel like reciting a mind-blowing hour of your own affirmations.

Once you've got your tape, play it as often as you like, but try to do it for at least twenty minutes a day for twenty-eight days. I know this sounds like a massive commitment but psychologists have discovered that the brain accepts new ideas over this time span, i.e. a moon's cycle. Don't worry if you miss a day, just add them on, and don't worry if you can't keep track of the days either. It is meant to be fun, not a worrying chore, and you will be helping your progress even if you're not completely systematic about it.

A subliminal tape

This is similar to the above except that the words are whispered just below the level of conscious hearing. The commercial tapes you can buy are made using sophisticated machinery, which means that the voice pitch is exact, but although home-made versions are much cruder, I have still found them to be brilliantly effective.

When you listen to a subliminal tape, all you hear with the conscious, 'listening' mind is soft music, but while this is happening, spoken messages are being received and absorbed by the subconscious mind. In this way your critical intellect, which might argue against these new possibilities and freedoms by reminding you of your failures and insecurities, is bypassed. Without this negative block, your deepest self can accept these new instructions and act on them. I shall give you some examples of how this can work, but first:

How to make your subliminal tape

You need two machines. Maybe you already have a large stereo or a small personal one. What you must have is at least one machine that records. If you don't have the right equipment, perhaps you can borrow one or enlist the help of a friend.

When you have your machines, you need to select a piece of music that appeals to you. It should be soft and soothing to put you in a relaxed frame of mind. Any of the New Age ones from the specialist shops mentioned in the Appendix and available by mail order are suitable if you like them, or use soothing classical pieces by composers such as Bach, or Pachelbel's *Canon*, or whatever relaxes you. Rock music is too stimulating and has too many messages of its own, including destructive ones about love.

When you have found your music, play it on one

machine and sit with the other recorder a few feet away. Hold the microphone – or if it is a hand-held recorder, the whole machine – at arm's length and speak your affirmations quietly. You will have to experiment with this so that you can just about hear the sibilant sound of your voice but not the actual words.

The result will not be a work of art! But it will most certainly be effective and what is more, unlike a tape that you have bought, all the affirmations will be tailor-made for you.

Of course, you don't have to put just your love affirmations on it. If you are working on prosperity or your body, you can include these as well, so that you have a personal tape that covers everything you are trying to bring into your life.

A friend's experience

One friend of mine married a man who regarded all women as potential conquests and had managed to seduce a good proportion of them. Her self-esteem was low enough when she finally walked out on him, but it plummeted even further when every man she met seemed to do the same thing: flirt and seduce other women. Then she discovered rebirthing – a breathing technique designed to release old programming – and how to use affirmations to create new thought patterns. She was in such a state that none of it seemed to work very well, so together we made a tape.

She played it for twenty-eight days and nothing happened.

Approximately two weeks afterwards, she started to come across all sorts of men who found her very attractive and asked her out. She met them in shops, garages, in the street, in cinema foyers and restaurants. It was all very flattering and heartening, except that not one of them was what she was looking for.

The problem was that she hadn't made a blueprint.

Not only did she then write one down as suggested

on p. 52, she also put it on a subliminal tape.

The result was that within a matter of weeks John entered her life, loving, faithful and as keen as she was to have a permanent partner.

Another friend's experience

This friend is happily married but was encouraged to make a tape just to see what happened. She stated all the things she wanted, including love. Several of her affirmations stated that she was gorgeous, sexy and desirable, that she was a magnet for the opposite sex. She actually treated it all as a huge joke.

Last Christmas she went to help out as a waitress at a hotel that was desperate for staff for its extra functions. One of these was for an all-male dinner to celebrate a company's successes and the waitresses were expecting trouble.

All of them, except my friend and one other woman, were young girls, mostly students and mostly with lovely bodies and faces. One of them even glanced at my friend – who is actually very good-looking – and muttered, 'I see they've wheeled in the geriatrics to help out.'

However, it was my friend who ended up being chased around the tables, who was propositioned for parties later in the week, who was asked by umpteen men what time she would be finishing work.

When she got home, her telephone started to ring. Several of the men had got hold of her number and began to pester her. It went on for several days until she realised that the tape might be the cause. She decided to change the affirmations to prosperity ones only.

The result: her husband left his job and bought a business. This has been so successful that they now live in a large house with several acres of land where they keep ponies for their children and for giving rides at local charity events.

The Last Word

There is no one in the world quite like you. You are uniquely attractive, charming and deserve a good love life. You can create and attract anything you want, so open up and begin to live.

4

Take Control of Your Marriage or Long-term Relationship

'Choose your life's mate carefully. From this one decision will come 90 per cent of all your happiness or misery'

H. Jackson Brown Jr.

Your marriage or partnership lines are the horizontal ones found on the cusp of the hand beneath the little finger and above the heart line (fig. 4.1). Whereas affection lines represent links with someone who you are fond of or even madly in love with, partnership lines represent a commitment like marriage or living with someone for a long time.

A long-term relationship will nearly always be represented by both affection and partnership lines. In the last twenty to thirty years, marriage lines have begun to show permanent breaks on them. Before that marriages tended to end only with the death of a partner.

Figure 4.1 shows some of the most common patterns. Again, any discrepancy between right and left hands will reveal a great deal about the frustration and commitment in a person's life.

In figure 4.1, line (a) is deeply etched, clear and straight on both hands, and represents a good, long-lasting partnership.

Line (b) is clear on the left hand, meaning that the

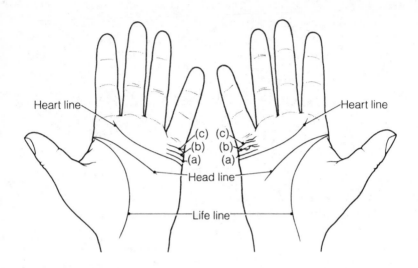

partnership has the potential to be a long-lasting relationship, but on the right hand is islanded and feathery.
Many people have this pattern when the relationship is
basically good but is being upset by a previous partner
and children or other family problems. Unless a break
appears on the lines, the partnership usually survives.

Line (c) begins on the left hand with a fork, which often
means either a choice between two partners or indecision
about the relationship due to other causes such as career
or family. If the line develops clearly after the fork it
means that once the choice or decision has been made
the relationship should be a good one. If, however, a
break appears on the right hand, as it does here, this
means that although the partnership has all the essentials
for durability, something has happened to upset it.

A break on a right-hand line nearly always represents
a separation or divorce. An examination of the affection
lines will show if someone new has arrived in the
person's life.

If you are the injured party, i.e. you have a break showing on your marriage line and it is your partner who has strayed, there will often by disturbances on the lifeline such as islands and worry lines – vertical lines running from the lifeline towards the Saturn finger (the middle, longest finger). These will be dealt with more fully in Chapter 5.

It is very interesting to note that in a good proportion of people with broken marriages, the left-hand line is intact and only the right is broken. If you have this pattern it means' you are breaking away from a relationship that could have lasted. Because the left hand reveals your true self, you are actually setting yourself up for a great deal of difficulty if you ignore it.

This pattern also shows that there is a dichotomy in your mind about the partnership; that part of you is still attached to it. This can create a backlash that surfaces in future relationships. If there are things you were meant to learn from the partnership difficulties but you have chosen to run away from them, those lessons will come up again in another form. This failure to learn from past experience is one of the reasons why some people keep attracting the same type of person over and over again.

There is another important point here. If you are the instigator of a breakup and your partner is deeply hurt, his or her pain can produce a psychic backlash.

Brain waves are energy. A brokenhearted partner will transmit massive disturbance into the ether, and this will reach the ex-partner via the bond they once shared.

In this situation, the broken-hearted partner will have strong, clear partnership lines on his or her right hand, and possibly also on the left. The breakaway partner, however, *always* has a broken partnership line on the right hand. I have seen many cases where a marriage has been through the divorce courts and the 'injured' partner has no sign of a break on either hand because he or she has never let go.

If either you or your ex-partner has these patterns it means that there is unfinished business in the relationship.

You can clear it up consciously or you can leave things, in which case you will find that those energies that have been stirred up by the break will create situations in your life that will ultimately resolve the problem. However, it may not be easy and I have seen it take years, even decades.

Now let's look at how to deal with specific problems, starting with relationships that have failed, then moving on to how to improve one that is faltering, and finally looking at how to make an already good relationship better.

Dealing With a Partnership Break

If your hand reveals the breakup of a partnership, it is possible to improve things and form a new, bridging line, but you should first check the affection lines running across your life-, head and heart lines to see if you are likely to succeed. If your affection lines are favourable, showing strong lines on the left hand as well as the right, then it is certainly worth trying to salvage or resurrect the partnership and work through the difficulties. If the affection lines are weak on the left hand but strong on the right, however, it means that you have been deluding yourself for a long time and it is time to take a long, hard, realistic look at your relationship. Despite your best efforts, if your partner is determined to break it up, you may be wasting your time.

But take heart. Although we may be in a lot of pain, we are meant to learn from poor relationships so that we have a better experience next time, just as Vicky and Eleanor did in Chapter 3.

In a partnership we enter into an agreement, usually tacit and often subconscious, that beneath all the romance and passion we are going to deal with the raw edges of ourselves, those longings and needs that want to find confirmation and union in another human being. In fact, the beginning of a partnership often feels like coming home; we feel a sense of relief that someone really loves us 'as we are'.

The root of all sexual relationships is the search for something beyond ourselves that will complete who we are. We long to give ourselves totally in love; and long for the ultimate in orgasm, sometimes known as the little death because it pierces both the ego and total physicality. If the relationship fails, we are forced into feeling scared, lonely and rejected, unattractive and not sufficiently lovable.

However, through many years of observing patterns of life, love and destiny, it has become obvious to me that every single one of us creates what happens to us. Each infidelity, each disappointment, each joy has been set up by us, through our doubt, our lack of self-confidence or our positive attitude. (More about this lack of self-esteem in Chapter 9.) The way to put things right and deal with rejection is to fill all those gaps ourselves. Here's how.

Make affirmations

Here are a few affirmations to build up a damaged heart and self-image. Insert your first name after the opening 'I' and fill the blanks with your partner's name:

1. I—now release all feelings of loss, despair and loneliness
2. I—am wonderful, loving and desirable
3. I—now accept that—has gone and release my need of him/her
4. Someone much better than—is now entering my life and I am totally fulfilled
5. I now release all anger and jealousy about—
6. —is past and my new life is beginning right now
7. Everything is working out for the best
8. I—am daily happier and more fulfilled

At first you may not feel that anything is working for you, but it is rather like trying to push a car: the initial force needed is great, but once it is moving, momentum helps it to gather speed.

Bring touch back into your life

Touch is the main thing that goes out of the window when a relationship ends. Just like the baby monkeys mentioned on p. 45, you are deprived of the touch, smell, and sight of your beloved. If your lover has gone or is on the blink, then sex will almost certainly have taken a nose dive either in quantity or quality. Sex is the ultimate touch, using nearly every nerve on the skin surface. For women, the lack of internal stimulus often gives rise to temporary health problems. The sense of loss can be as sharp as a dagger, so you must cosset yourself. Instead of feeling worthless, you should make up for what you are missing by getting yourself in shape and making appointments for treatments where touch is paramount. The following suggestions will help you whether the problem is a relationship that has ended or one that is going through a difficult patch.

Visit the hairdresser It can be completely soothing to hand yourself over to someone kind but impersonal who washes and massages your scalp, who brushes and preens your hair. Not only will you feel better, you will look better too.

Have a massage We are gradually moving out of the nudge, nudge, wink, wink attitude towards massage. It is becoming big business, and rightly so. A full body massage will stimulate the skin and the lymph pathways. It will release knots in muscles and disperse the buildup of lactic-acid crystals which impede the circulation and are painful. And, of course, help compensate for the absence of touch in your life at the moment.

Visit a chiropractor Making sure that your general skeletal structure is in alignment helps to keep the nerve, lymph and energy pathways clear. It helps your health and, again, someone is touching you. It is a physical affirmation: you are telling your body that it deserves to function well and feel good, and because of this it will begin to respond in a positive way.

Visit a reflexologist   Reflexology is a deep foot massage that relaxes and stimulates all the organs of the body, helping to normalise their functions. We tend to neglect our feet and this can be a good way to restore a sense of balance and 'earth' ourselves.

There are many more body treatments such as shiatsu, acupuncture, rolfing, etc. which can be found in the classified advertisements of health and exercise magazines as well as in the specialist bookshops mentioned in the Appendix. Make sure that your reflexologist or chiropodist is a registered professional.

Live as if you had a partner

It is important to assure yourself that either your love will come back or you will find someone new and better. But don't do this with a sense of emptiness. Use your affirmations. You are still attractive. Either you are in the process of attracting a new love into your life or you are doing exciting new things in the interim.

Turn it all into a joyous, anticipatory process. Buy yourself your favourite foods. Set the table as you would if you were having a cosy tête-à-tête with candles or music or whatever creates your favourite ambience.

Don't just sit there alone moping. Make it a physical affirmation. Say to the universe that this is the way you want to live with a partner.

Do the things you would like to with a partner. Go to the cinema, the theatre, your favourite restaurant. Go for walks, swimming or whatever you would like to do if you were living with your ideal partner.

You can always take a friend, of course, but remember that you are in fact saying this is what your ideal date would be. The two examples which follow might not have had such successful results if a friend had been present.

David's story

David's hands showed a weak left affection line and a

strong right, and his partnership lines were frayed. Sure enough, after one year together his girlfriend left him for another man, so he decided to get himself together and improve the weak pattern of feathery lines that was emerging.

First of all he decided to change his image. He had grown careless about his dress, often wearing old jeans, so he bought himself some good new clothes. Then he decided to make a date with himself at the cinema and then at his favourite bistro.

Every time he caught himself feeling it was unnatural to be alone, he told himself that this was a new beginning and that he was creating an avenue along which a new friendship could arrive.

Well, it worked that very first day. His waitress at the bistro commented on his mournful expression. David muttered something about being on his own and she invited him to a party later that night. Of course he went and a whole new circle of friends opened up for him.

During this time, the lines on his hands began to change. One of the feathery lines on his left hand began to strengthen, followed by a similar pattern on the right. Within eighteen months the woman represented by these lines arrived in his life and they have now happily settled down together.

Jenny's story

Jenny had a good job as a secretary in a computer company but it didn't fulfil her. She craved glamour and thought she had found it with Tony, a freelance journalist who travelled the world and took her to parties with highly placed and well-connected people.

Both her hands showed feathery affection lines and broken partnership lines, indicating that this was not a match made in heaven. However, Jenny refused to believe this until one day Tony just upped and left.

Angry and bitter, she decided to follow the procedures

outlined above, but never got as far as a first date with herself. The dishy chiropractor asked her out instead.

The affair lasted several months, during which time she discovered a deep interest in his work and her own considerable healing powers. As a result, she is now a fully qualified chiropractor with an up-market clientele and a social life that fills all the gaps that Tony left.

Be adventurous

Often the affairs that feathery affection lines represent are designed to show us something about ourselves, and if we can overcome our sense of loss, anger and bitterness, they will lead us to fuller lives.

Of course, it's not always this quick or easy. Sometimes it takes a little while to build up your confidence again, especially if you are still in love with your 'ex' and hope that he or she will come back.

In addition to making dates with yourself and giving yourself as good a time as possible, a gap between relationships is a good moment to do all those things you've longed to do but felt were impossible while you were together.

A trek in the Himalayas? Now is the time to do it. White-water canoeing, horse-riding in the Sierra Nevada, flamenco dancing in Andalusia, seeing the treasures of Italy, hanging out in Mexico, hill-walking in Scotland? Get your tickets and go. The boost it will give your life will be worth every penny and every doubt. It will also open up the avenues for change.

Bob's story

Bob's partnership lines on the cusp of his hands were islanded and frayed. His affection lines across his life-, head and heart lines were frayed on the left hand and strong on the right, indicating a great deal of self-delusion. Furthermore, on both hands his lifeline broke about ten years into his marriage and branched off to join the fate line, indicating a major trauma (see Chapter 5).

Bob's had been a long and difficult marriage. In the beginning he had adored his young wife. Anne was totally different from the apparently sedate and boring wives of the people he saw around him. She was willing to try anything. If he suggested a weekend trip to Italy, she would drop everything and go. When he wanted to go to the United States, throwing job and caution to the wind, she gave up everything as well and went with him.

But Anne wasn't ready for the humdrum daily life of marriage, and it wasn't long before she began to have lovers – lots of them, and most of them much younger than Bob. She made no secret of it and the more Bob put up with it, inwardly hoping that she would get it out of her system, the more she flaunted it. Finally, however, he decided he'd had enough and he threw her out to live with her new young lover.

Bob felt very sorry for himself, feeling hard done by and calling his wife the villain of the piece. What he could not see at the time was that part of his personality needed the excitement and challenge that such a flighty partner would bring, and, like so many of us, he had been naïve enough to think that he could tame her.

Well, what Bob was advised to do now was to give himself what he wanted from a partner. He had no difficulty attracting women. He found them everywhere – in pubs, restaurants, squash clubs, swimming pools, and at dinner parties. Most of them were out for a good time, not wanting commitment, and he got through so many that it left him breathless with amazement.

It was some time before Bob realised what he was doing, but finally he saw that he was behaving exactly like his ex-wife: the more the merrier. He had never wanted a humdrum life himself, which was why he had chosen a wife like Anne.

When Bob was giving himself what he wanted, he was acting out the repressed part of his personality that had been damaged by his marriage. It restored his confidence and equilibrium, and he is now happily settled with a lively woman whose idea of a good time is like his – physical challenges like sailing and mountaineering, not a succession of lovers.

And Bob's ex-wife? In her early thirties, after a complete rave during her twenties, Anne settled down with the staidest of men, but he also happened to be a good provider, giving her luxury and security – things that had never been on Bob's list of priorities.

What to do with a Failing Relationship

So you have a partnership line that is islanded and feathery. You will be experiencing the difficulties it brings in a variety of ways. Are you:
    bored?
    frustrated?
    hemmed in?
    miserable?
    desperately unhappy?
    having an affair?
Is your partner:
    ill-treating you?
    ignoring you?
    out all the time doing his or her own projects?
    failing to understand you?
    being unfaithful?
    Don't worry. It's your life and you can change it. As you change, so will your partner's reactions to you. Then you can decide whether the improvement is what you want.

Put the excitement back into your life

If you are bored and frustrated, what is it that you feel you are missing in your life? Money? Travel and excitement? Progress in your career?

These things may not be entirely your partner's fault, so set about improving them yourself.

Start to improve your *finances* so that you have enough for the luxuries or fun that you want.

If your partner doesn't want to travel to the places you do, decide that it is your right to go, even if he or she doesn't want to. The problem then is that you will end up arguing about the rights and duties of a partner and who should be compromising, and/or feeling depressed that you are not travelling on an adventure together. In other words, if you go at all, you will probably be going alone.

Only you can decide how important it is to you, but the fact is that too many compromises for the sake of your partner will lead to deadness and it would be better for you to make a stand and book your holiday, change your job or whatever it is that is bugging you. The result will be that you will feel more alive, and your partner will have received a clear message about where he or she stands. Your partner can then either stay at home or come with you.

Change a negative set-up

If you are ill-treated either verbally or physically, or your partner is being unfaithful, why are you putting up with it? Are you hoping that things will get better, or are you too frightened to make a move?

You can make things get better. Some people refuse to change, and your partner may be one of them, but you *can* change yourself. Whatever it is that instigates the abuse, start to avoid it, and decide whether your relationship is worth it.

Jane's story

Jane was married to Peter. She had a strong line on her left hand showing that she had a good bond, and a feathery line on her right hand indicating difficulties.

The marriage line on the cusp of her hand was strong to start with, islanded in the middle, then continued in a strong, clear line.

Her problem was that she had a successful career but found it difficult to be meticulous in the house. Although it was clean, it was often untidy with magazines, papers and correspondence, whilst the kitchen table was littered with shopping, packets of cereal, the breadboard and crumbs.

Peter, however, was house-proud. His mother, who had never worked, had always kept her house immaculate. He resented Jane's refusal to make housework a priority and was constantly nagging her. He made a token effort to help but essentially regarded it as a woman's job.

Things went from bad to worse. Jane saw red over the nagging and Peter turned to violent verbal abuse. He called her a slut, dirty and lazy, a stupid, illogical woman. The final straw came when he sprang a dinner party for some Dutch distributors for his company on her. She was at work and only had her lunch hour to buy food and a couple of hours at home to prepare it. She asked Peter if he would just run the hoover over the carpets. He flatly refused, saying that it was woman's work.

Jane threw down all her cooking utensils, took off her apron, told him that since the dinner was in aid of his career he could cook it and entertain his guests himself, got in her car and drove off to stay with a friend.

Peter couldn't cope. He took the Dutch people out to dinner. But Jane didn't return. As far as she was concerned Peter was showing no regard for her situation and very little affection. He was decidedly unlovable, demanding and spoilt.

During her absence the kitchen was piled high with shopping, unwashed dishes and pans. The bathrooms were uncleaned, there was a mountain of washing. Peter couldn't iron properly so his precious business shirts were creased. He himself looked tired and ill. He missed Jane terribly and begged her to come back.

Jane decided to give him one more chance, and it

worked. He helped her as much as he could and they employed professional help once a month to give the place a blitz. Shortly afterwards, Jane became pregnant. She is now running a successful business from home.

Develop your own interests

If your partner is out all the time, what is he or she doing that is so interesting? Is he playing golf or squash, or going out with the boys? Is she going to concerts, having lunches with her girlfriends? If it is honestly nothing that intrinsically threatens your relationship, like being out on the town looking for conquests, you would do better to look at yourself.

Are you putting your all into your relationship, wanting your partner to be meat and drink to you, wanting his or her very soul? Often in the beginning both partners want this, but it tends to fade and it is rare to find it lasting very long. It is a sign that passion has come down to earth, but if you are a passion junkie you are going to have withdrawal symptoms and find it difficult to cope with your partner having other interests.

The way out is to develop your *own* interests again, to pick up where you left off before you became involved, to go for some of those secret ambitions and become the interesting person your partner fell in love with.

Don't court disaster

If your partner is being unfaithful, the marriage lines on the cusp of the right hand and possibly also the left will invariably be islanded or even broken when this is happening, and the affection lines on the right hand will become very fragmented. But please note: if you have such a pattern, it does *not* necessarily mean that your partner is cheating on you. This pattern also represents other kinds of difficulties.

If you can see such a pattern before you get married, the advice is definitely to be aware of what you are letting yourself in for. If you have broken marriage lines on both hands, then you are literally courting disaster and it would be a good idea to look deeply into yourself to see why. Such patterns often appear on the hands of people who have an almost self-destructive quality.

Typical problems with such a configuration are a desire for perfection or a tendency to be drawn to attractive, exciting people who don't want commitment. One woman with this pattern had an extremely handsome, loving husband who was highly placed professionally. She drove them into the divorce courts because she felt that her own career was inferior and wanted him to boost her self-esteem. She repeated the pattern with a succession of potential partners – always attracting and choosing men of high professional standing and always feeling inferior. Her marriage lines only strengthened when she began to do some deep work on her feelings of inadequacy and her lack of self-esteem.

Making a Good Relationship Better

So you are in a good, permanent relationship. You have fairly solid-looking affection and partnership lines on both hands. You're committed to your partner or spouse and you're either blissfully happy or just jogging along, coping with day-to-day routines, the mortgage, bills.

Well, you can make things better still and firm up those lines even more.

Getting your own life in order will have a magnetic effect on your partner. The stronger the bond between you, the better the result. Anything you do that makes you happier – barring infidelity – will improve your partner's life. By being true to yourself, you can strengthen an already good bond.

Improve your finances

This is obvious. If you have more money coming in

as a couple, you can have more fun. Writing your own prosperity affirmations can help your partner's magnetism as far as prosperity is concerned too.

One young woman had achieved a fair amount of success with her prosperity affirmations, but then stopped for a while. A few days after she had begun again, her husband came home from work saying, 'You've been doing those affirmations again, haven't you?' He was grinning from ear to ear. He had won £200 on a company sweepstake, and £1,100 on a football sweepstake! (See Chapter 2 for a full explanation of techniques.)

Improve your body and health

This, too, is obvious. If you have been dissatisfied with your appearance for whatever reason and finally do something about it so that you feel vital and confident, your partner is naturally going to feel the change in you. Be aware, though, that at first he or she might be suspicious of the reason for the new you.

I had one friend whose husband got uptight because she started to paint her fingernails. He didn't believe that after twelve years of marriage she could be doing this for him, or simply to express the joy of being alive and to make her hands more attractive. He soon got the idea, though. He began to come home with flowers and chocolates for her as if she were a new girlfriend.

Build up your self-esteem

The more you honour yourself, the more alive you and your relationship will feel. Begin to treat yourself as the centre of your universe – which you are – and your partner will begin to pull up alongside you.

Initially, a reaction may set in. Your partner may have become rooted and stuck, and may not like the subtle changes that signal your emergence from the rut. It can take a little time and sometimes a bit of rough going for him or her to shake loose too.

Resolve work problems

Work can be a huge problem area in a partnership. Forty or fifty years ago everyone knew their place: the men went out to work, the women stayed at home. The woman's place was at the kitchen sink.

Women's difficulties   Nowadays most women expect to work, which can lead to all sorts of difficulties. Problems can arise if she suddenly decides to leave her job to look after the children, if she changes her job to have more time at home at a lower salary, or if she suddenly becomes a high-flyer.

The answer is to honour yourself at all times, to trust your intuition.

If you talk it over with your husband or boyfriend and he is really bothered by your longing to 'drop out' or go for a promotion, you must still trust yourself. Not to do so will lead to a slow dying of the fire within you and a simmering resentment against your partner that will affect your relationship.

If money is the problem, work on prosperity (see Chapter 2).

If the type of work is the problem, for example your hours are unsocial or you have to take trips away from home, you should still go for it. A good partnership will weather it and be richer for the expansion.

Men's difficulties Traditionally the man has been expected to be the main breadwinner, which is a heavy burden. Many times I have seen enthusiastic young men become dull and soured by the drudgery of having to maintain a certain income level to support a family and mortgage. Mortgages and the high price of property in this country can spell death for romance.

If you suddenly want to take up golf or flying or scuba diving and your wife or girlfriend is pointing out all the pitfalls and expense, trust your gut feeling – *do it*. Life is for living and sharing.

There is a detailed exercise for finding your dream in Chapter 5.

The Last Word

There is only one person in control of your life: you. In the deepest part of your psyche you are unique and wonderful and others want to know and blend with you. The more you allow this deep, true self to emerge, the more love and friendship will flow smoothly into your life. So release the barriers, relax, and let it come to you.

5

Take Control of Your Longevity and Your Body

'There is a spirit which is pure and which is beyond old age and death . . . This is Atman, the spirit in man. He who has found and knows his Soul has found all the worlds, has achieved all his desires'

Chandogya Upanishad

Most people are familiar with the lifeline. It starts between the thumb and forefinger, curves around the mount of Venus, and ends somewhere near the wrist (fig. 5.1).

The lifeline is probably the single most important line of the hand. It reveals the quality of your energy and the periods in your life when you might experience difficulties and those when everything is smooth and expanding.

It can also indicate when you expect to die. Please note the word *expect*. There is no predestined, fixed time when your 'number is up'. That idea is man-made. If you *believe* in it, however, that is what will happen.

Finding your Life Expectancy

Find a moment when you are not going to be disturbed and sit down. Just relax for a few minutes, making sure that you are comfortable, and then close your eyes.

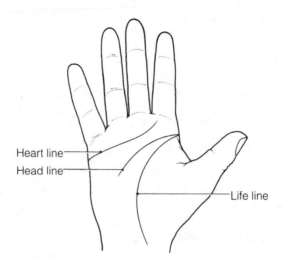

Now just ask yourself at what age you think you are going to die. Not a nice thought is it? But I bet that without much effort on your part, there is a decade zooming into view, and your lifeline will reflect that image.

Are you happy with this picture? Does it seem so far away at the moment that it doesn't matter? Or have you a short lifeline that is worrying you? (Incidentally, a short lifeline does not necessarily indicate a short life, as you will see.)

Whatever is there on your hands is there because your thoughts put them there. As always, if you don't like it, you can change it. First, though, you need to be aware of some of the thoughts that have helped to cause the problem.

A good many of us have patterns on our lifelines that come from our family background. Members of the same family often seem to wipe themselves out at around the same age. Many times I have seen the thirtysomething child, niece or nephew of someone who died at the age of fifty-six, say, show a lifeline beginning to weaken at about the same point in their own life. With only a small amount of help to change their thought patterns, their lines quickly strengthen and potential problems are averted.

Equally, longevity can seem to run in a family. Although sometimes we have a genetic tendency towards certain illnesses such as heart trouble, we have to remember that each one of is unique. We are not Uncle John, Mum or Dad, and we live in a world in which life expectancy is increasing all the time.

Against all this, however, a lot of elderly people, and some not so elderly, often say, 'I don't want to live to be a great age.' Whether they feel that this is somehow a noble sentiment showing their lack of fear of death, or whether they dread being incapacitated, I am not always sure. In any case, it is time to stop thinking that advanced years mean illness and infirmity. As soon as we stop thinking in this way as a culture, our lifelines and health will be vigorous into old age.

For a lot of people the rot seems to set in around thirty to thirty-five, which is absolutely ridiculous when at that age we are still young, with youthful skin and bodies. I have lost count of the number of times I have heard, 'I'm thirty next birthday. I'm absolutely dreading it.' This is said with a groaning voice and genuine bewilderment that life is passing so quickly.

The reason for this is programmed thinking. Our society builds these ideas into us. They are reinforced every time we see things like

'Veteran footballer over the hill at 31.'
'You need this anti-wrinkle cream at age 27.'
'Actress aged 32 and still *looking good'* (as if she ought to be a wrinkled hag.

Job advertisement – *'preferred age 25–35.'*

The result is that we become paranoid about our lives when we should still be out there go-getting.

Life spans are becoming much longer. I have seen some people aged between eighteen and twenty-five

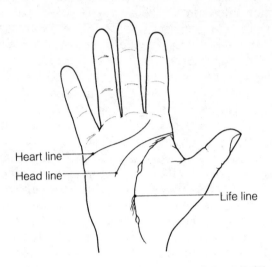

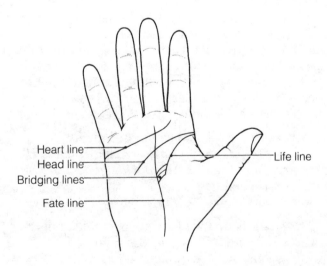

with lifelines curving right around the base of the mount of Venus, indicating a life expectancy of 110–120. Of course, this isn't much good if your health is poor and your lifestyle is limited, so we shall take a look at all these aspects and see how to improve them.

The Quality of the Lifeline

A lifeline that is clear, well etched and a good, deep colour indicates good health. A weak and feathery or islanded and pale lifeline (fig. 5.2) indicates a lack of vigour and problems that could lead to health difficulties. As with the indications for prosperity and love, the two hands are often different and the cause is always thought patterns.

Sometimes the lifeline appears short, breaking off about two-thirds of the way down the palm. This is generally compensated for by the fate line. Usually there is a bridging line attaching the fading lifeline to the fate line, the latter carrying on strongly up the hand (fig. 5.3).

When this pattern appears it means that there is a huge trauma. The person's life is breaking away and continuing along another path. Divorce or a relationship break-up are very often the cause of such a pattern as they can temporarily affect the health. Often, however, the new line is much stronger, as if the life force is regenerating itself after the trauma and developing into something more fulfilling.

If this pattern appears on the right hand but not the left, as is quite frequently the case, it means that the situation was not actually determined by mental patterns developed in childhood. It is more a reflection of the social and cultural patterns of the moment. Our rocketing divorce rate is due to us demanding more fulfilment, and it is interesting to note that the majority of these divorces are initiated by women. The liberation movement that began to take hold in the seventies and eighties is

largely responsible for these changing hand patterns.
The right- and left-hand lifelines of older people tend
to be much more uniform.

A break in the lifeline that is supported by another
line (fig. 5.4) means that there could be some trauma
or illness, but that the problem will be overcome. The
same is true of a series of feathery lines (fig. 5.5, (*a*))
or a clear line (fig 5.5,(*b*)) accompanying the lifeline
along its path will act as an insurance against illness
and accident.

Whatever the lines on your hands tell you, the following techniques will enable you to reassert control over
the quality and length of your life.

Changing Your Attitudes

Over the years I have seen several people go from good
health to serious illness and back again, and observing
them has supported the concept on which this book

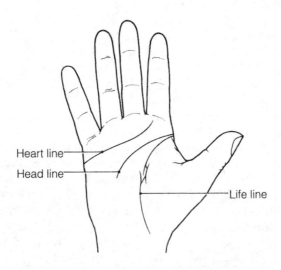

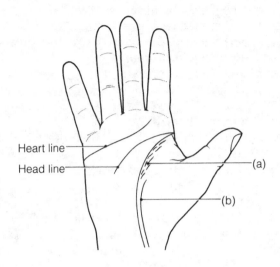

is based: that everything in our lives is created by our minds.

As you begin to make positive changes in your life and you begin to see changes on your hands, don't worry if a new line appears on one hand and not the other. As a general rule, if the new or deepening line appears on the right hand it means that you are making a conscious effort with something and most of your friends and family will be aware of it. If it appears on the left hand, it means that the change is at a deep, inner level, that you have shifted some long-held belief or ambition.

Stephanie's story

Stephanie was robustly healthy, though very overweight, the result of oversensitivity and comfort eating after a failed marriage. Her lifelines were long, clear and strong. Only the marriage lines on the cusp of her hand revealed trauma, with a series of islands and a break.

I had seen her intermittently over several years, but just before Christmas a few years ago the lifeline on her right hand began to break up at the age she was then – thirty-two. Her marriage was over and the divorce just through, but she had discovered that her husband had been abusing her eldest daughter.

She was racked with fury and frustration. She wanted to kill him and could find no outlet for her rage. No amount of counselling would help her to understand what she was doing to herself.

Six months later, the upper half of her right-hand lifeline had disappeared. She had been diagnosed as having breast cancer that had spread like wildfire through her lymphatic system. The consultant had been brutal with her and told her that she had less than six months to live and that she had better get her affairs in order.

However, Stephanie's left-hand lifeline was still strong and she knew enough from listening to me over the years to realise that the consultant might be wrong, and this gave her hope. She set to work with affirmations and

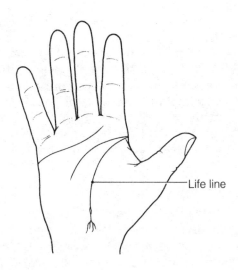

Life line

visualisations, a purifying regime for her body and a scanning and boosting technique for the endocrine glands (see pp. 116-119). Although she had to undergo major surgery as well as chemotherapy, which left her weak and ill, she persevered with every technique to try to get herself well.

Three months later the consultant said that his prediction might have been premature: she had perhaps two to three years.

One year later he pronounced that her cancer was in remission.

Stephanie is still alive and well. The lifelines on both hands are as strong as they originally were. She has lost weight and has also done some work on releasing and forgiving her ex-husband (see pp. 124–126 for techniques). This was essential to prevent the same resentment building up again to affect her health.

Banish negative thinking

Quite a few of us do, at some time or other, become ill, and for many people this tendency increases in later years and is reflected in a lifeline that starts to break up with little dots and feathering (fig. 5.6). This is not 'predestined' or 'fate'; it is the result of a lifetime of thinking that you're going to leave the planet at a certain age, often around the time that certain members of your family did.

How many times have you heard people, especially family members make remarks like:

'The one thing you can be sure of on this planet is that you will die.'

'Time and tide wait for no man.'

'When your number's up, that's it.'

'When he pops his clogs . . . '

'When I conk out.'

'Nothing lasts forever, we all just wear out.'

'It comes to all of us one day.'

Given the prevalence of this type of thinking, it's

hardly surprising that we tend to believe that old age means infirmity and decay.

If you were asked to describe your thoughts on being told by someone that he or she had a relative of ninety-three, the chances are that you would have immediately conjured up an image of someone wrinkled, bent, arthritic, slow and generally lacking in vitality.

Because so many old people do end up this way, it has become embedded in our psyches that this is what extreme old age means. But it doesn't have to be this way. I know a woman in her eighties who still makes an annual trek to the Himalayas, and another in her early seventies who only experienced the menopause five years ago. Both of these women, it is interesting to note, live in remote mountain areas in the British Isles where they are not bombarded daily by the ideas and busyness of town and city life. They do not have the herd instinct.

With regard to the late-menopausal woman, she is married but she and her husband decided to give up on sex several years ago. He was beginning to find it exhausting and she was perfectly content to go along with this. In every other way, both have happy and fulfilled lives. The decision released her from having to think about her menstrual cycle in terms of possible pregnancy and the need for birth control.

In fact, she never gave her cycle a thought until she went to stay with a relative who lived in a large city. Because she was menstruating during her stay, the relative was shocked, convinced her that something was organically wrong with her and persuaded her to go to the doctor.

From then, it was a downward spiral. She began to dwell on it and within the space of one month she was plunged into full-blown menopause.

The point to this is that we are all the products of our cultural thinking and when we really and truly believe something about our bodies, that is how it will be. It sometimes needs quite a lot of courage and perseverance to winkle out all those subversive little thoughts, but the following affirmations will help:

1. My body is perfect, whole and healthy for the length of my life
2. Illness is a negative thought. I—release all such thoughts right now
3. My body was designed to be strong and healthy for ever and I allow this design to continue my entire life
4. My parents and grandparents made their own choices about life and death, but I—do not have to follow them. I live as healthily and as long as I want

Of course, you can make up your own affirmations if you feel it is appropriate. Above all, be careful what you say in daily life. Built into our language are certain key phrases like:

'She hasn't a leg to stand on.'
'He's a pain in the neck.'
'You get up my nose.'
'It really twists me up.'
'I feel choked about it.'
'I feel gutted.'
'You need that like a hole in the head.'
'He'll be the death of me.'
'He's dead cool.'

The point is that our subconscious mind doesn't differentiate between a true affirmation and a sarcastic comment. If you are always using phrases like the above you are setting yourself up for some physical trouble.

Suzanne was caught up in a difficult domestic situation and kept saying, 'I just don't have a leg to stand on.' Within a couple of months she broke her ankle. Coincidence? Possibly, but just watch and see how such phrases work out in your own life.

Getting in control of the aging process

Even today, in our so-called advanced times, death is a taboo subject. When we are young we put the whole idea to the back of our minds and feel that we have loads of time before it need ever enter our consciousness. But for a lot of people doubt seems to creep in around the age of thirty-five to forty, when they begin to take stock and make plans to achieve more fulfilment and success, or to slow down and prepare for an easier time for what they believe will be the second half of their life.

In their fifties a lot of people seem to be almost in despair, as if they are pushing against the incoming tide. In reality, everything I have observed over the years points to the fact that those very thoughts of despair are not only slowly killing them, but also preventing them from enjoying the present.

I have given affirmations and visualisations to people in their twenties whose lifelines are breaking up at around the age of fifty to sixty with startling results. Although they may have come to me with a love or career problem, they have combined techniques to solve the initial problem with work on health and longevity, and as a result their lifelines have smoothed and lengthened.

Interestingly, their lifelines have usually responded much quicker than the lines to do with their main problem, and I am sure that this is because they have no strong emotional energy thwarting their progress in this area. In other words, if they are mainly concerned with a love difficulty but they are doing a few longevity affirmations just to please me, they are worrying about love but are not especially bothered at this stage about longevity. This is the key. *Whatever we worry about and anxiously dwell upon grows and takes ages to shift.* The things we love or are light-hearted about respond rapidly to any change we impose upon them.

Affirmations for increased health, vitality & longevity

1. I—now release all my ideas about death and dying
2. I—am not my family. My body does not have to obey family patterns. I live as long as I want, as healthily as I want and in the way that I want
3. I—am whole and free and perfect
4. No doubt or negativity can ever stop me from achieving my purpose
5. I—release all doubt, all stress, all anxiety
6. Each time I—feel stressed, my body and mind sort it all out perfectly
7. I—need never worry about stress. It is released the moment it occurs
8. Stress is no more than a light breeze in my life, ephemeral and unimportant
9. My body now purifies itself of all toxic waste
10. I—am now led to the perfect exercises and practices to heal and cosset my body

Reinforcing Change

It is highly probable that at this stage some of your innermost doubts and fears about aging and dying are coming to the surface. The following exercise will help you to deal with your own particular situation and can be used for other aspects of your life as well.

Access your alpha brain-wave rhythm

Normally, when we are awake we are in the beta brain-wave rhythm (the thought patterns we develop during this state of consciousness are the ones revealed on the right hand). The alpha and theta rhythms are the deeper ones we contact when meditating or in the moments between sleep and waking. These are very creative, intuitive states.

Very often we surface from sleep with our dreams and the deeper desires or problems contained in them resonating in our mind. Brilliant new ideas can often come from achieving this state.

Meditation, where the alpha rhythm is regularly reached, is traditionally passive, using a mantra (repeated word or sound) or contemplative theme. People who regularly meditate or access by other means the brain's alpha levels for approximately twenty minutes a day have been shown to slow down or even reverse the aging process. High blood pressure has been reduced, cardiovascular activity has become more efficient, the nervous system's reaction time and the hearing threshold have been improved, and scores on intelligence tests have increased, as have mental agility and accuracy and long-term memory.

Although meditation is very effective, it is possible to access the alpha rhythm by the following exercise. Whilst the focus in this exercise is on healing and longevity, it is important to remember that you can use it for anything you want to improve in your life. A shorter version of this technique is included on the tape with this book, but you may like to record your own so that you can include your own affirmations at the end.

The technique

Step 1   You need to find a time and a space where you will be quiet and uninterrupted for about twenty minutes. Switch off the telephone and decide not to answer the door.

A slightly darkened room is best – half-draw the curtains during the day, or use soft lighting at night. You can either sit in a comfortable chair that also keeps your spine straight, or you can lie down. You could use a bed, but if you feel that you will be inclined to fall asleep, use the floor.

You must be warm, so unless the temperature is around 70°F or higher, cover yourself with something warm like a duvet or sleeping bag.

Step 2   You must be as relaxed as you possibly can be. Some of you may be familiar with this traditional yoga technique. The important thing here is to do only as much as feels comfortable. It is your body and it knows how much is good for it. If you feel you have done enough, just stop. Making a decision to stop is empowering in itself and you will benefit from it.

Starting with your feet, curl your toes towards your instep with as much tension as possible. Imagine you have a squash ball in your instep that you must squeeze as hard as possible. Feel the tension in your calves, your knees, thighs and hips. Take the squeeze right up your body to your face and eyes. Squeeze tight and hold for a count of five, then relax, letting go and flopping onto the floor or into your chair.

Next squeeze your buttocks together, pulling up on the pelvis as if you are trying to pull all your lower internal organs upwards. Again, take the squeeze up your spine, into your arms, shoulders, neck and face. Squeeze and hold for a count of five. Relax, letting go completely.

Now suck in your abdomen as if you are trying to touch your spine. Take the suck upwards into your arms, shoulders, neck and head. Hold for a count of five and then relax, breathing out long and deeply.

Next, squeeze your upper chest, shoulders and arms inwards – from back to front for your chest, and in towards your spine for your arms and shoulders. Take the squeeze up to your face, screwing it up as if you want to scream. Hold for a count of five, and release.

Lastly, concentrate on your face. Screw up your eyes and open your mouth wide as if all the tension in your life is being forced out. Stick your tongue out as far as you can. Feel the squeeze in the back of your neck and throat. Hold and release.

Let yourself go floppy like a rag doll. Just sink onto the floor or into your chair and take several deep breaths.

Now slowly count backwards from ten to zero, taking

a deep breath at each count and relaxing more fully as you go.

When you reach zero you should be nicely relaxed. If you are not already in the alpha rhythm, you will be getting pretty close. Don't worry if you still feel tension in some places. This is as far as your body wants to go today and that is absolutely perfect for you. It is your body and it is your best friend. If it is showing resistance, just be aware of where you feel this resistance and be kind to it, as a parent would a child with a bruise or a sore place.

Step 3   Close your eyes and let thoughts come and go if they want to. If you spend the first five minutes thinking about something else like what you're going to have for dinner tonight, that's OK. This is what is uppermost in your mind and if you are easy with it, or find you resolve some problem around it, the thought will eventually go away.

Breathe easily and rhythmically. When you breathe out, just release the air as if you were making a long sigh and pause for a count of two. When you breathe in, take in the air as if you were sniffing a flower and pause for a count of two. Repeat this several times.

Step 4   When you feel nice and relaxed, take your awareness to any area that feels troubled and begin to 'breathe' into it.

Let us suppose that you have a headache. Take your awareness to the pain and begin to breathe soothing air towards it. Some people like to introduce a healing colour such as turquoise or purple but any colour that appeals to you or spontaneously presents itself to your mind's eye is the right one for you. Breathe in the air as if you were smelling a flower surrounded by your colour and say to yourself that your head is now healing itself and that your immune system is now dealing with any stress in your body.

Now take your awareness to any other part of your body that is feeling under par and do the same thing.

If you are basically feeling quite well, this is a good

time to fill your body with energy and light, to see each part of it – your limbs, heart, liver, kidneys, brain, circulation, etc. – functioning at its optimum.

At this point, you can also mentally say any affirmations that you are currently working with. Their effectiveness will be enhanced by your quietened state. They do not need to be just about health. If you are working on relationships, prosperity or self-esteem, this is the perfect time to introduce the ideas to your relaxed brain.

Step 5   Now that you are as relaxed as you feel you can be today, we are going to work a little on your health and longevity.

Your cells contain your genes, but they also contain the knowledge of your thoughts. Your thoughts are an integral part of your nervous system, of your whole structure. At a profound level your thoughts sustain your cellular structure and your cellular structure sustains your thoughts. They are a complete unit and through your thoughts you can improve any damage to your structure.

Your cells were designed to be perfect and everything in this book is designed to reassert that perfection.

You were designed to have a beautiful, strong body that allows you to fulfil all your dreams of comfort, sharing, creating and joy. Take a moment now to see that perfection. See your body as you know you want it to be and as it actually is at a profound level.

See yourself in the lovely circumstances you know you really want.

See yourself fulfilling that creative spark inside you, whether through creating new ways of doing things, through working happily for someone else, or through being at home with your children.

See yourself sharing your life with the people you want.

There is nothing to stop you.

In this place, in this space in your head, is where your future is being moulded.

Mould it into the shape you would like now.

Give yourself as much time as you need for this.

Now take yourself forward to the next decade of your life.

Does your life seem diminished in any way? If so, something in your ideas about aging is the cause. Take a moment to correct this. The next decade of your life is as vital and fulfilling as any, perhaps more so because of your increased knowledge.

Take yourself forward again to the following decade, that is twenty years from where you are now. How does it feel? A bit scary? Or are you raring to go? Does it feel as if being twenty years older might diminish you in some way? If so, who says so? Newspapers? Magazines? Or are the people you know who are twenty years older than you not so vibrant? Certainly, some of them are full of joy and vitality, but generally the tendency is for people to appear to 'sink' a little as they get older.

Take a few moments to see yourself twenty years older but even more attractive and vital than you are now. Your body is superb and your health perfect.

Now you are going to take a much bigger leap forward in time. You are going to see yourself at one hundred years of age. One hundred years.

How does it feel? More importantly, how do you look? Your image is almost certainly based on pictures you have seen of old people celebrating their centenary with their families and friends. Usually they are white-haired and frail. You are now going to change this image. See yourself aged one hundred with a full head of natural-coloured hair. See the pigment flowing from the root along the hair shaft and the hair nourished by a vigorous circulation.

Now see yourself rise out of your chair like a twenty-year-old and move around greeting people. Your body is strong and straight, your bones full and firm. And what are you doing with your life? Not sitting in front of the television wondering which moment is going to be your last, I hope. Are you planning to learn another language? Are you looking forward to reading some of the new books coming out this year? Are you up to date with new computer techniques? Maybe you would like to take a full-time course at a college or with the Open University? Best of all, you could think of earning some money with a job. Just think of it: an army of one-hundred-year-olds with all their faculties intact, offering their ideas and wisdom through some form of work. In other words, are you still full of vitality and living in our world?

Give yourself as much time as you need for this.

Step 6   When you feel that you have done enough, rest quietly for a few minutes and allow more normal, everyday thoughts to resurface. You might find it easier to say to yourself that your session is now finished and that you are going to open your eyes in a few minutes. Don't attempt to open your eyes fully at first – just squint and then close them again. Do everything slowly. Give your body time to adjust to its normal, waking state.

Benefits of contacting the Alpha Brainwave

In a study on the effects of meditation on the aging process, R. K. Wallace took forty-seven subjects who practised transcendental meditation and TM Siddhi techniques (see Appendix for further information) and compared them with a control group of people who didn't meditate. The average age was 52.8. He used the Morgan Adult Growth Examination, which gives reliable indicators of biological age.

Wallace discovered that biologically, those who had been meditating for up to five years were 7.1 years younger than their control-group counterparts, whilst those who had been meditating for five years or more were fifteen years younger than controls of the same age. Four of the meditators were twenty-seven years younger biologically than their opposite numbers in the control group.

Although I could give numerous examples of people

looking years younger than expected as a result of these techniques, I think the experience of two of them, Wendy and Sandra, gives a good idea of the power of the mind over the aging process.

Wendy's and Sandra's stories

Both women were forty-five when I first met them and were very close friends. Sandra was happily married with three children; Wendy had two children but was divorced and living with her new boyfriend. Wendy had been a community nurse for twenty years and was quite forceful about her belief in the medical lessons she had learned as a student nurse twenty-seven years earlier. Sandra was a chiropodist and was much more open to new ideas. Interestingly, their lifelines were very similar; quite vigorous until about the age of 50, after which they became islanded and feathery.

After I had given them both the alpha technique, I met them by chance at a party. Wendy became quite aggressive about it, saying that it was mere self-hypnosis and nothing could stop the aging process. She said that at her age her body was preparing for the menopause and that was that.

Sandra, however, was very taken with the technique and was using it regularly. She was using the relaxation technique and then mentally saying her affirmations or visualising. Although both women were attractive, there was a glow about Sandra's skin, a fresh-faced youthfulness. She had also noticed changes on her lifeline. Whereas before it had ended weakly, it had now become strong and pink and had grown another centimetre in length.

Some time later, I met Sandra on her own. She was worried because Wendy never let a conversation pass without discussing her age and physical changes, and her negative state of mind was affecting Sandra. Apparently Wendy kept talking about the menopause, and Sandra was sure that, like a negative affirmation, it was affecting her own cycle. Wendy, however, simply scoffed and said that Sandra just couldn't accept that she was undergoing the change of life.

I gave Sandra some affirmations to counteract these negative ideas and suggested that she keep Wendy at arm's length for a while.

A few months later I received a letter from Wendy. She was in hospital recovering from a hysterectomy due to a fibroid. It was not a serious condition and she had been given the choice of having the operation or leaving it for a while, but her rigid ideas had made her fearful of leaving anything to chance. As she herself wrote: 'I realise now that I talked myself into this. I have no choice now – I am in full-blown menopause whether I like it or not.'

As for Sandra, she continued with the techniques and her life simply took off. Her husband received a promotion together with a hefty pay rise, whilst she herself moved out of the NHS to become a school matron, which fitted in with her family life. At the age of forty-nine she became pregnant again, and just before her fiftieth birthday gave birth to a healthy baby boy.

Although having such a late baby would not be everyone's choice, it fulfilled Sandra and today, in her fifties, she not only looks a good fifteen years younger than her 'real' age, she has the vitality to match.

Results for healing

Let's suppose that you have been dealing with toothache. It is possible that the decay is too far gone for you to heal completely at this stage, but in one of his workshops, Leonard Orr, the founder of the rebirthing technique, healed a woman when a large filling came out. She trusted him implicitly and the tooth just grew back whole. *So it is possible*. It's a question of trust and belief. You simply have to start trusting yourself. The more you practise the technique, the more powerful and easier it becomes.

Sometimes the technique works in an oblique way. I tried it myself for a filling that was loose and 'leaking'. Because my dentist at the time believed in leaving things well alone unless something major needed to be done, I began to worry that something was going wrong underneath the filling.

I used the technique and could feel energy moving around the area, bringing about some improvement, but then I had a powerful impulse to change my dentist. I chose one of the most reputable – and also one of the most expensive – dentists I knew of, who also had a formidable team of hygienists. They found that the trouble was not the tooth at all but a deep pocket in the gum that needed antibiotics. Within hours not only was the troublesome gum sorted out but my whole jaw was treated and healed.

Possibly, if I had trusted enough and persisted enough, I would have improved my immune system to the point where it would have healed the pocket of infection itself, but at the very least using the technique got me doing things that promoted healing.

One complete success I have had using the technique was to heal a raging sore throat that had already begun to develop into a heavy, flu-like cold.

I had an appointment I was anxious to keep, but feeling as I did, I thought I would have to cancel. So I set to work, lying down and relaxing as I've already described and breathing steadily into the sore throat, becoming aware of its rawness.

First of all I told it to go away. I imagined the soreness as lots of little devils scraping their forks on it and I bombarded them with the feeling of loathing they conjured up. I began to swear at them and I realised that anger and frustration was one of the emotions that had weakened me in the first place.

Then I imagined a pink light surrounded by gold and 'breathed' it into my throat, holding my breath for a few seconds and then releasing. At this stage I could actually feel the energy moving around my throat, but it doesn't matter if you don't feel a thing: your intention is what counts. I then introduced a soft, cooling sky-blue edged with gold because this seemed to be what I needed to cool down the inflammation.

When you use this technique, all you need to do is to choose the colours that you love the most or which suddenly, intuitively seem best for you. Don't worry if you only get a vague feeling of colour or almost nothing at all, the technique works just as well if you say to yourself: 'I am now breathing in soft pink edged with gold.' Your mind's knowledge of the colour will do the rest.

This technique can be used for life-threatening illnesses too. Stephanie (see p. 94) used it for her cancer three times a day. Not all of us have the time for this kind of commitment, but Stephanie's life was in the balance and she wanted to give herself every possible chance.

In the next chapter we will take all this a stage further. From healing illness and our ideas about life expectancy, we will go on to look at creating optimum health and vitality.

The Last Word

Everything in your body and in your life is controlled by your thoughts. At a profound level your thoughts and your cellular structure are an indivisible unit. Your body and life are as good as your thoughts will allow them to be, so raise your thinking. You are beautiful. Your body is strong and perfect. You can do, be and have anything you want.

6

Allowing Your Perfect Body
to Emerge

'We are not just bones and blood and flesh, we are
magnificent conduits of energy'

Chris Griscom

The human body is a perfect machine, the human brain
more sophisticated than any computer. Unfortunately, not
only do we fail to use nine-tenths of the brain's powers,
we distort the body's perfect blueprint with stress, negative
emotions and unhealthy lifestyles that lead to accelerated
aging, obesity and illness.

Although the lifeline is the main indicator of vitality,
there are other areas of the hands that reveal problems. We
will take a look at these and then at exercises that can help
you achieve the perfect machine for living life to the full
– your body.

Reading Your Hands

Angry red blotches on the mount of the Moon (fig. 6.1,
(*a*)) reveal that the lungs are in trouble in some way. This
sign very often shows up on the hands of smokers. I have
seen the blotches fade a little as the result of cutting down,
but they don't disappear until smoking has been given up
completely.

If you don't smoke and you have blotches, it means

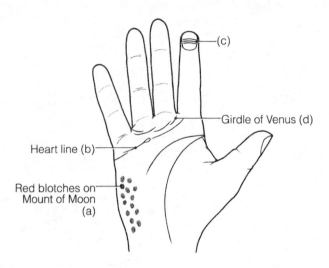

that there is not enough oxygen in your bloodstream. You may be suffering from a heavy cold or cough, or you may be very tense and stressed, which is making you breathe shallowly. The blotches are a clear warning to start taking care of yourself. Introduce more aerobic exercise into your lifestyle to free up your tense diaphragm and lungs, and get yourself a medical overhaul.

If you have no cough or bronchitis and don't feel the need to see a doctor, it's a good idea to consult an alternative practitioner such as a reflexologist or acupuncturist to balance your body.

The heart line

The quality of the heart line can also give an indication of the state of your circulation, but it must be read in conjunction with other lines before a conclusion about your health can be drawn.

As a general guide, a strong, clear line means a strong

pump, whereas a pale, fine line can sometimes mean a weaker constitution that does not respond well to strain and exertion. If your heart line is feathery and broken up at any point (fig. 6.1, (b)) it means that you could be under severe stress and your heart could be taking the strain.

In the case of heart trouble there is usually a dot or island or break on the heart line beneath the mount of Mercury. However, other lines on the hand have to support this, so it is important not to become anxious if your lines seem weak. Bridging lines will form to show that the danger has passed.

Sometimes such patterns reveal severe stress caused by the pain of a broken love affair. Although physical heart problems are unlikely, it shows that you need to be looking after yourself.

Horizontal ridges on the nails (fig 6.1, (c)) indicate a shock to the system. Usually they are the result of emotional stress or physical illness, and as the nails take four to six months to grow from moon to edge, it is possible to date the trauma fairly accurately. However, I have seen one or two people with permanent indentations. These are not the same thing, and are probably caused by some accidental damage to the nail bed.

The situation that caused the ridges may appear trivial – I have known people to develop them just after Christmas when long-standing resentment of in-laws and other relatives has surfaced – but they are a warning that your body has registered the problem as a trauma and you need to take care.

If you know that your body is reacting badly to situations like this, you must look after yourself. Here's how.

Dealing with Stress

Although I firmly believe that the mind controls everything, and that you can create the ideal life and body for yourself simply by programming it properly, if you are under stress it is a clear signal that your mind has temporarily lost its usual control. If this is the case, it is a good idea to boost yourself with vitamins and supplements. These will help to tide you over until you get back on course.

What follows is a brief summary of the supplements that I have found to be particularly helpful at times of stress.

Supplementing your diet with B vitamins is one of the first lines of defence against stress. The supplement I like best is American Nutrition's Strezz B Vite because it also contains minerals that aid the absorption of the vitamins and works on a timed-release principle so that your body is protected throughout the day. It can be found in some chemists and in most health-food shops. Brewer's yeast tablets are also good as long as you don't have a sensitivity to yeast.

A great deal of research is being done on antioxidants, showing them to be an important factor in healing stress damage. Their function is to mop up free radicals, which are highly reactive atoms or molecules that can form toxic peroxides which can damage and destroy cells. Stress, poor diet, environmental pollution and exposure to sunlight can all lead to free-radical activity. In extreme cases they can lead to the formation of cancers, but in all cases they contribute to the breakdown of body tissue, leading to the development of sagging skin and wrinkles.

The most well-known antioxidants are beta-carotene, which produces as much vitamin A as the body needs, and vitamins E and C. If your diet is rich in fresh fruit and vegetables you are probably getting enough antioxidants anyway, but if you are under stress, a supplement would be helpful. Good and reasonably priced sources can be found at most large chemists and health-food stores.

Bach flower remedies are also helpful for combatting stress. Their rescue remedy is an all-purpose pick-me-up, but for specific remedies applicable to your state of mind, you need to refer to their leaflet. Bach remedies can be found at some large chemists and most health-food stores.

Homeopathic remedies are helpful for many types of illness and if the cause of the ridges on your nails is bereavement – whether through the major shock of death or the deep emotional upset of a failed relationship – Aconite can be helpful. For prolonged mourning, Ignatia is recommended.

If you want to use homeopathic remedies, a small book-let describing the remedies and the particular symptoms they relieve is available from most health-food stores.

Incidentally, you don't have to wait to see if ridges are forming on your nails before you take action with supplements. If you are feeling stressed, use vitamin supplements, homeopathic and Bach remedies to prevent the symptoms from getting worse.

Achieving Optimum Health

Most of us live our lives under par. We are subjected to mental stress at work and at home, emotional stress from relationships, and physical stress from environmental pollution, noise and too much or too little exercise. The conscious mind is aware of this, so we buzz around like a mouse on a treadmill feeling that we have to put up with it.

Our inner selves know otherwise.

The endocrine glands are the powerhouses of our body. They secrete hormones that regulate our bodily functions. The master gland of the endocrines is the pituitary gland, about the size of a pea and its essential hormones control growth, the development and balance of the reproductive organs, thyroid function, the islets of Langerhans in the pancreas, and the adrenal cortex. The other major glands that control our life functions are the parathyroids, thyroid, thymus, adrenals, pancreas, and the reproductive glands (the testes in the male and the ovaries in the female). Most of the time our awareness of the functioning of these glands comes from their results: menstruation and pregnancy when functioning is healthy, for example, or water retention, sluggish metabolism, or brittle bones when functioning is poor. The glands can just tick over, sometimes getting kicked off balance so that we become ill, or they can function at a super-level to produce optimum health.

The health and balance of the glands is revealed in the hands by fairly clear life- and heart lines, and by the colour of the palms. A clear, healthy-looking colour indicates a balanced system. A deep angry colour can indicate emotional anxieties, which can lead to imbalance, whilst a yellowish colour can indicate nervous and emotional blocks. Quite often our hands can be revealing an imbalance, but we have become so used to it that we think it is normal.

The fact is that the essence of life itself revolves around these glands and it is possible to make conscious contact with them to promote optimum physical health. This contact also puts you in touch with your intuitive awareness, a faculty practically half asleep in the Western world.

Your body is your powerhouse. It can bring you everything you want and need for your journey through life. The following techniques will assist you in all your goals.

Opening the intuitive awareness of your body

If you have a friend to read the process out to you and you feel like sharing it, all well and good. Otherwise, most people dictate the process onto a tape and play it back. Both methods are effective.

Step 1   If you can, it is a good idea to use the technique for reaching the alpha brainwave rhythm, as described on p. 100. If you don't have time, however, it is enough to relax as fully as possible. Breathe deeply, as if you were smelling a flower. Hold for a count of two and then release. Let the breath out in a long sigh and again hold for a count of two. Take several of these deep breaths and then count backwards from ten to one, relaxing more at each count. Now become aware of your body, of your diaphragm moving up and down as you breathe, of the way it all just holds effortlessly together except where there is tension.

Be aware of what a wonderful machine your body is. It is perfect. Your brain is more powerful than any computer. This is your chance to begin to use it.

Step 2   Take your awareness down to the soles of your feet. It doesn't matter if you are lying down, be aware of their connectedness to the earth. Through the soles of your feet you make a daily connection with the forces of the earth, even if those forces are covered by layers of concrete. Be aware of this connection now and try to get an impression of how healthy your feet are.

Does this area of your body seem dark or troubled, or is it just nondescript?

You can improve your energy by sending your awareness to this area in the form of light. This can be a white or golden glow, or it can be a colour if one appeals to you. Something may arise spontaneously; if so, use it.

Don't worry if nothing comes and everything seems grey. Your *intention* will do the trick just as well, and as you grow more skilful at this process you will begin to sense the energy in your body in ways unique to you.

Step 3   Move your awareness up your body to your knees. Be aware of the wonderful job they do of supporting your entire frame and weight to keep it balanced and upright. Again, sense this area of your body:

Does it seem depleted in any way?

Or is it ticking over nicely?

In either case, send your thoughts of health and vitality down in the form of a golden or silvery light or whatever seems appropriate to you.

Step 4   Travelling upwards again, concentrate your awareness on your reproductive area – the testes if you are a man, your ovaries if you are a woman.

We tend to be much more aware of activity in these areas and you may, therefore, find it easier to visualise or sense them:

Do they seem dark or grey or depleted?

Or are they fizzing with vitality?

Send healing energy to them as before, or if you find this difficult, just send your thoughts. You can even use an affirmation such as: 'My reproductive glands and organs are in total health and harmony.'

Step 5 Move up to the pancreas. Sense its position behind your stomach and be aware of the important work it does for your metabolism. Again check it for balance and send it energy.

Step 6 Do the same for your adrenal glands, which lie above the kidneys.

Step 7 Move to the heart area, where the thymus is situated. Some schools of thought state that this is not very important in adults as its function tends to lessen from childhood onwards, but others feel, as I do, that it has an active role to play as part of the immune system.

Check it for balance and depletion and bathe it in light. You may find the glands nearer the head slightly easier to sense; if so, make a mental note of this so that you can recapture the sensation more easily for other areas.

Step 8 Do the same for the thyroid gland, which is situated at the base of the neck.

Step 9 Now move your awareness to your forehead and slightly back into the brain to sense the pineal gland. This is the area of intuitive awareness and is sometimes called the third eye. It lies dormant in many people and this exercise can stimulate it, making life richer.

Repeat the process of checking it for balance, trying to get an awareness of the area:

Is it dark or apparently non existent?
Or do you have a distinct awareness of it?
In either case, send balancing energy.

Step 10   You may be feeling a bit tired or bored by now, but hang in there. The pituitary gland at the base of the brain is one of the most important glands in the body and it needs your attention.

You may get a strong sense of aliveness from this or any of the other glands. If so, note how this feels and allow it to spread and fill the area. If the area feels depleted, energise it with your thoughts as before.

Step 11   Last of all, try to imagine the healing, balancing energy you have been using surrounding you from head to toe like a cocoon. This helps to connect the entire magnetic field of the body and will give you energy.

You may feel tired or woozy after completing this and not very energetic at all. Some people have emerged feeling angry. Don't worry. It is a sure sign that you have achieved something, that you have relaxed parts of your system that have been under par or tense.

If you have half an hour to spare, lie down for a while and relax. Bring yourself together afterwards with a cup of weakish tea or decaffeinated or instant coffee. Filter coffee is a bit too much of a jolt to the kidneys after a balancing technique like this.

As a matter of interest, in areas known for the great longevity of their people, for example in Asia Minor and Tibet, a good, long-leaf tea is a staple drink and believed to contribute to a long and healthy life. Modern research is beginning to support this too. Good buys are green teas such as gunpowder or jasmine, or China Keemun or Earl Grey, which has the added benefit of bergamot oil, said by aromatherapists to be useful in the prevention and cure of cancer. If you are intent on boosting your health, you might like to incorporate these into your daily diet or at least when you are having a health-promoting time.

Discovering the physical effects of our words

Muscle testing is a wonderfully simple technique for discovering our innate strengths and weaknesses, and will show you how easily you can either sabotage or enhance what you feel and do with words. You need a friend to help you. In fact, it works even better if you have a group of friends who can try it on each other.

Stand up and place your left hand over your heart area while holding your right hand out as firmly and rigid as possible.

Then say either to yourself or out loud: 'I am brilliant, strong and fearless. There is nothing I cannot do.'

After you have repeated this two or three times, your friend should push as hard as possible on your right arm. The chances are that it will remain where it is, showing that you are physically strong.

Now repeat two or three times: 'I am a weak, bumbling fool. I fail at everything.'

See what happens when your friend pushes on your arm.

In nearly every case I have seen, the arm flops down like a bent reed.

If by some fluke you find that it doesn't, it will be because you are actually saying to yourself: 'I don't believe in this mumbo jumbo. My arm will stay where it is.' In this case, your mind is still controlling your body. Positive thoughts create positive physical responses.

You can also use muscle testing to test the strength of your endocrine glands to enhance your health still further. For this, place your left hand over the area in question. For the:

- pituitary – the top of the head
- pineal – the forehead
- thyroid – the throat
- thymus – the heart
- adrenals – the solar plexus
- pancreas – the abdomen

- ovaries or testes – the pubic bone

When your friend tries to push down on your extended right arm, the relative strength or weakness of the gland in question will be obvious. You can do the appropriate exercises or visualisations to strengthen them.

Debbie's story

Debbie had just lost her father, and as an only child was under immense strain to support her mother. Her lifeline had developed an island and she was experiencing pains in her knees.

When she did this exercise her feet and legs seemed almost lacking substance. Instinctively, the colour red flooded her mind and she visualised sending this into her feet. Her legs seemed like jelly with no support at all, so she mentally inserted props and splints and a cooling, soothing blue colour. She also felt that she ought to be eating more carbohydrate foods as her eating habits had become so erratic.

Within hours, the pains in her legs had disappeared, and she began to organise her life more positively. She also began to experience a new, lighter energy that made her feel better than she had ever felt before.

Tone up your body

This physical exercise gives a good, all-over boost to the glands and the body, but if you are in any doubt about the advisability of trying it, especially if you suffer from high blood pressure or heart problems, it is a good idea to check with your doctor first.

Stand up straight, feet together, shoulders relaxed and down. Breathe easily.

Raise your arms above your head, fingertips touching. Stretch up gently, and then over to your right as far as you can go without straining. Hold for a count of five. Now come up straight and repeat to the left. Again, hold for a count of five.

Put your arms down by your sides and breathe easily for a few moments.

Now raise them again and gently stretch backwards as far as you can go. You will probably find that your head goes back further than your arms and that is all right. You are giving your spine a good stretch and stimulating all the glands along your trunk.

Come up gently and relax, your arms by your sides.

Now bend slowly forward from your waist, tilting your head back slightly to protect your spine.

Bend down as far as you can go, allowing your arms to rest near your feet. Let your head flop and find its own level. Keeping your legs firm and straight, let yourself sag and go loose like a rag doll. Let your mouth hang loose, your jaw, your cheeks. Hold this for as long as it feels comfortable.

Now come up and stand easily, breathing gently for a few seconds.

Fresh blood will have flowed into your neck, shoulders and head, revitalising the glands and organs there.

Doing this simple routine a few times a week, along with any other regular exercise, will help you to feel really well, and when you feel good your self-esteem will automatically begin to rise.

Eat super-foods

Many excellent books have been written about the importance of certain foods for good health. The following is a summary of one or two main points.

First of all, a body cannot perfect and heal itself if it is carrying a toxic overload from stress and environmental pollution, so an emphasis on purifying foods such as fruits and vegetables is important, especially when we are under par.

There is also a considerable body of research indicating that the colour of natural foods is significant, and that different colours correspond to different endocrine glands. Some of this knowledge comes from Eastern traditions.

Briefly stated, colours and parts of the body correspond as follows:

Red   = connection to the earth, feet, legs, survival instinct, sexual organs
Orange = sexual organs and pancreas
Yellow = solar plexus, adrenal glands, kidneys
Green   = thymus, heart
Blue   = thyroid, throat
Indigo = pineal gland, eyes, ears, nose
Purple = pituitary gland, brain

In our natural state, our intuition would usually attract us to the foods we need to balance our bodies, but in industrialised societies we are losing touch with this instinct. If we know we are under par in a particular organ, therefore, it can do no harm to apply these principles.

For example, love and sex play such a vital role in our lives, so let's say that you want to enhance your sexual function. Red and orange are the colours that correspond to the pelvic area of the body, so go for red apples, tomatoes, carrots, strawberries, raspberries, red and orange peppers, and oranges.

To enhance your kidney function, vegetables and fruits in the yellow colour spectrum, corresponding to the adrenal glands, are appropriate. Bananas, for example, are high in potassium, whilst melons are a natural diuretic, both enhancing kidney function.

Traditional Chinese acupuncture emphasises that if you have an aversion or passion for a particular colour, then you may have an imbalance that the eating of particular foods can help to normalise. For example, if you hate the colour red and never wear it, you may have a lowering of energies in the corresponding organs that by eating red foods and wearing red colours, even if only in underwear or a tie or scarf, you may help to adjust.

Similarly from Eastern traditions comes the idea that if you have been overworking and are feeling a bit spaced out, now is a good time to eat meat and root vegetables to 'earth' you. Conversely, if you have been feeling heavy and stuck and much too earthed, eating things that grow high up like some fruits can lighten you. You may feel that this cannot apply to you and that's fine. When you feel ready, you may like to try it to see what is most effective for you.

Usually, our seasons do it all for us. In the summer we tend to feel light anyway, with sunshine and lighter clothing accompanied by cooling salads and fruits. In winter, when we need the warmth, we eat heavier, stodgier, earthy foods, wrapping our bodies up against the elements.

If you are trying to bring a creative project to life and are floundering, you may find it helpful to take this into consideration. In the summer we tend to be inspired, but it is not always easy to get down to the nuts and bolts. The dark days of winter are a much better time for beginning the process of making ideas real. During this period we can act as if we were a bulb, quietly germinating, working on our 'creation' in a down-to-earth and practical way, honing and perfecting it until the spring and summer, when we can burst out and bring it properly into being. This applies to our bodies, our work, our loves and lives.

If you are feeling stuck over anything, just drop it if you can – for example if it's work that's worrying you, put your worrying aside – and let the seasons and your intuition take over until you are ready to take up the reins again. This is a way of getting back in touch with the natural rhythms that urban living and industrial demands have obscured.

Learn to forgive

If you are anything like me, the first time someone tells you that forgiveness is the way to perfect health and rejuvenation you will probably want to run in the opposite direction. It smacks of penance and sack-cloth and ashes, not something that anyone at the turn of the century wants to be bothered with.

But, as you will probably discover, the truth is that unforgiveness is the cause of nearly every ailment you have, including obesity, and I don't mean just forgiving other people. The main person you need to forgive is probably yourself.

Forgiveness means releasing yourself from the negative emotions that are binding you to another person or situation, leaving you impotent and ensnared. It means freeing yourself so that your life can move faster into happier, more fulfilling and more prosperous directions. Try the following exercise to help you appreciate what forgiveness can do for you.

Forgiveness Exercise   Take a piece of paper and a pen and sit down somewhere you won't be disturbed for a while. Close your eyes for a few minutes and picture the one person you dislike most in all the world. What has he or she done to you?

Now draw a picture of this person. Make him or her as ugly and horrible as he or she seems to you. Draw as many jagged and angry edges as you need. Let your mind free-associate and put all your feelings into your drawing.

Alongside this drawing, you must now draw a picture of yourself. Put in all your feelings about yourself in relation to this other person. Make yourself as wretched and insignificant or as helpless as the situation makes you feel. Keep on drawing and free-associating until you have done enough.

Now look at what you've done:

- Are you smaller than the object of your feelings?
- Are you softer, more amorphous, less defined?
- Or are you wound up tight in a tiny ball?

Whatever you have made yourself look like, it is a distortion of who you really are and this is stopping you from getting where you want to go.

All these feelings are lying in your system, blocking up the works. All these feelings are a gigantic obstacle. You are wasting loads of energy on them, and you are the one who is suffering.

Silly, isn't it? No matter what this person has done to

you, you don't want to let your feelings continue to screw you up for years to come. You want to get on with your life and be happy, prosperous and successful. You need to let this garbage go.

Just look at your picture and say, 'You're not worth it. You're not worth all the effort I've put into you. I'm letting you go. I'm releasing myself from you. My life is brilliant without my feelings about you in it.'

You can say whatever you like; make up whatever words you like. If you don't want to speak them out loud, write them down on another piece of paper. You can free-associate again, concentrating on what you want your life to be like once you have rid yourself of these negative emotions.

If it helps, you can say things like, 'If it hadn't been for you I would have . . . ' and list the things you feel you have been prevented from doing or having.

Go on for as long as you need.

The life you think you would have had but for this problem is actually one of your next goals. *Go for it.* There is actually nothing stopping you except your feelings, so let this person/situation go now. *Release the problem and get on with what you really want.*

Tear up your drawing in a symbolic act of destruction of the old – you can even burn it if you like – and spend the next few minutes on planning at least one thing you can do to further the goals that this person/situation has thwarted. Realise that you are in control of your life. No one else. No matter what anyone tries to tell you.

You can repeat this exercise for everyone and everything that you feel upset about.

Sarah's story

Sarah was a classic example of the problems caused by not forgiving. She was married with two children, who were looked after by a series of nannies, and had started up her own consultancy agency, which flourished all through the eighties. However, she was so preoccupied with her work that her marriage began to suffer. Her husband finally left her for another woman and during the recession her business crashed.

Sarah was devastated. Her only compensation was her two children, but in spite of this she began to gain weight. She felt bloated and looked it.

At this point she decided to try the techniques I gave her. Several times she drew her husband and his new woman with so much hate that the pen scored holes in the paper. She also tried a forgiveness technique similar to the process on p. 125 in which she closed her eyes, relaxed and breathed deeply for about five minutes, then gently took her awareness to her feelings about her situation. Inevitably, the villain of the piece kept emerging as her husband.

She allowed herself to feel all her anger, hatred and bitterness towards him, often punching pillows as if they were his head. When she had exhausted the emotions and was quiet again, she was encouraged to see him as the loving man he had once been with her.

At first this was hard and it provoked screaming rage. (Rather than upset the neighbours, she yelled into a pillow.) This helped to release the residue of anger, but initially all she could say was: 'I hate him, I just hate him, and I'll never be able to forgive him.'

Because of this, she decided to leave this to one side for a while and concentrate on herself. She felt hard done by. She had worked all hours and thought that her husband should have been proud and supportive, so she allowed those feelings of pride in her achievements to surface and gave herself a pat on the back. This often resulted in tears, but she always felt lighter and easier afterwards.

She then took a look at her children. She knew that she had not given them much time because of her career, and she cried a lot for the sadness of it all. However, she was encouraged to see herself not only as having done the best she could, but now as being able to give them more of the time and care they had previously missed out on.

She looked at her career, felt the horror of failure, of

the loss of position and money, and even as she did so she spontaneously saw it as an opportunity for a new beginning.

Finally, she came back to look at her husband again and realised that he had put up with a lot. It didn't ease the distress of desertion, but at a deep level she began to put it into perspective.

She cried a lot for the loss of what they had once had. She still felt hatred and loathing for his new woman which she couldn't shift, so she began to affirm during her 'meditation' that she was now released from the situation and could make a fresh start.

All this took several sessions to work through and each time she said that she felt lighter in spirit. The excess weight began to drop off too. Over five meditation sessions she lost several pounds without altering the way she was eating.

Jane's story

We all have someone or something that bugs us – colleagues at work, an in-law, old hurts from childhood. Dealing with these often releases and frees us in surprising ways.

Jane felt that her parents had been mean with their money during her childhood. Her father was wealthy but had sent her to a state school and had never helped her financially in any way. He believed a woman's place was in the home and as a result actively prevented her from reaching her full potential in either education or career.

She still felt very bitter about her lost opportunities, so she decided to try these forgiveness techniques. In her drawing, her father was enormous and overpowering while she was small and meek and insignificant. She followed this drawing session with a visualisation session. She took herself back to several key moments when she felt her life had altered course because of her father. She allowed herself to feel all her resentment, breathing deeply into it and taking plenty of time to mull over incidents of her childhood.

After about ten minutes she had a sudden flash of insight and saw her father as a frightened boy who had struggled to build up his life from scratch. She was overwhelmed by this and all her real feelings of love rushed up. The forgiveness was spontaneous and total.

She deliberately behaved quite normally when she next saw him, but as she was leaving he handed her an envelope, saying, 'I've done rather well on the stock market just lately and I thought I'd like to pass it on to you.' Inside was a cheque for £10,000.

She could hardly believe it. Somehow her love and forgiveness had reached her father without her saying a direct word to him, something that often happens with deep ties.

Jane decided to use the money to finance a business-studies course her father had prevented her from taking a few years earlier. When she told him what she was doing, he told her to keep the £10,000 for herself and that he would pay whatever was necessary for the course.

Whatever your problems with parents or others close to you might be, trying these exercises will begin to release you. They probably won't produce hefty cheques, but they will certainly help you to progress, because forgiving your problems 'unsticks' you, releases you so that your life can begin to flow more easily in the way it was meant to. Your body will reflect the change as well, perhaps with lost weight if that has been a problem, or with a straighter back, a lighter step, increased energy.

Achieving Your Perfect Body

There cannot be any one of us who thinks that he or she has the perfect face or body. Even the most beautiful models will bemoan their big ears or their long nose or some barely visible defect. Many of these ideas come from childhood, when the smallest detail that could be caricatured by other children would be mercilessly taunted, or a teasing relative said something like, 'I see you've got the family nose.'

The truth is that most of us are walking around with a warped body image and not only can this be brought back to normal, it can be improved.

Improve your body image

We all have a magnetic field around us, sometimes called the kinaesthetic, etheric or light body, and by working with this, we can begin to effect actual physical change. Try the following exercise:

Step 1   You need to stand up for this but close your eyes. You are going to scan your body from top to toe.

First, be aware of your feet and how they are placed on the floor. Feel the floor and its relationship to your feet. How does the air feel against them? Are they warm? Cold? What shape are they? Long? Short?

Now sense your whole weight-bearing structure from your hips down to your feet. How does this feel in comparison with the rest of your body? Is there tension anywhere? What shape are your thighs? Your knees? Your calves?

Become aware of your pelvis, your hips. Their position in relation to the buttocks. Your genitals. The shape of you. Are you easy with yourself, or are you hunching over, hiding in some way?

Move up through your abdomen to your chest. What shape are you? Are you stooping slightly or straight-backed? How do your neck and head sit on your shoulders?

Move up to your face. How are your eyes positioned? Wide apart or close to the bridge of the nose? What shape is your nose and how does it look on your face? Your mouth, is it wide or small, full or thin? How does it fit in with the shape of your face?

Now cast your mind's eye quickly from top to toe, scanning up and down once or twice to integrate the details.

Step 2   The next stage is to see yourself as you feel

you would like to be. Really imagine your body as you would like it to look. Are you taller, slimmer or more muscled? See yourself as the beautiful being you were intended to be.

Now take this new awareness to each part of your body as before, starting with your feet and legs. See them as you really want to be. Move on to:

- Your hips and genitals
- Your abdomen and chest
- Your shoulders
- Neck
- Head

At this point you might like to see this beautiful body in some exotic setting, for example half naked on a tropical beach. Yes, this is you receiving all the admiring glances and wolf whistles as you emerge from the sea, the water cascading down your gorgeous limbs while a rum and Coke waits for you at a table with a bevy of admirers ready to chat you up.

Step 3   Now you must move into this 'new' body. You may have imagined it as all around yourself anyway, which is fine. If not and you have pictured it as standing somewhere in front of you, step into it.

How does it feel? A bit strange, or just right? Make any adjustments you like. Remember, this ideal body is as much a part of you as the real one is, and the more you do this exercise the more your 'ideal' body will become integrated with your physical form and you will begin to notice changes.

People have actually 'grown' up to one inch after only a week trying this exercise. Not having any medical data or equipment apart from a ruler for before and after measurements, we have concluded that either it is the result of straightening a spine that has been hunched up, or that mind over matter is omnipotent.

Other people have achieved weight loss and the removal of unsightly sags and lines, especially on the face.

Take exercise

So much has been written about exercise, there's no need to go into its benefits here, except to say that incorporating some form of aerobic activity into your weekly programme is best for a healthy life.

However, one form of exercise that deserves special mention is yoga. This Eastern system of stretching and toning exercises is now very mainstream and has far subtler and wide-ranging effects than Western forms of exercise.

Yoga stimulates and activates the endocrine glands and their electromagnetic counterparts in the chakras of the subtle body, leading to optimum health. Because of this, it has been called a rejuvenator, and I have known people with grey hair return partially or fully to their normal colour from performing the inverted postures, and older people who are slowing down begin to regain some of their youthful vitality. Most local authorities run yoga classes and your library would have details.

Achieving Your Perfect Face

All faces have the foundation of beauty in them, but most of us seem to concentrate on our imperfections. Any feature that we feel is not quite as we would like it to be can be improved by turning our *loving* attention towards it. By 'loving attention', I mean the opposite of feeling pinched and negative when we look in the mirror. The more we feel negative about a feature, the worse it will begin to appear; the more we begin to work on improvements, feeling confident in the outcome, the better it will gradually become.

Make affirmations

Either write these out or say them out loud when you look in the mirror.

Visualise

You can combine this quick technique for the face with any of the passive visualising exercises in this book. Use it after the exercise you have chosen, when you will be relaxed and in the perfect state to get good results.

Very few of us escape some fine lines around the eyes or face or a crepiness of the neck, even as early as our twenties. This exercise helps to erase existing lines and prevents new ones from forming.

Let's suppose that you have some fine lines beneath your eyes or crow's-feet from smiling. Take your awareness to them and see them being gently plumped out and flattened until the skin is once more firm and resilient.

Choose which area(s) you want to work on and work out some appropriate affirmations. For example, you may want to create a firmer jaw line and could use statements such as:

1. I—am now creating a strong, firm jawline
2. My—jawline is now firming and perfecting itself
3. I have no doubts about the perfection of my—jawline
4. Every day my—jawline is firmer and more perfect

You can repeat the process for any part of your face, for example grooves around your nose and mouth.

You may feel energy moving around them straight away, but results will be just as good even if you don't. It depends on your body's awareness of itself which will become more acute the more you use these routines.

Colour can be very useful at this point, if it appeals to you. Pink is the traditional shade to use for the contours of the skin and face. As with the healing technique mentioned in Chapter 5, visualise pink in your mind's eye and then 'breathe' it into the area you are trying to improve, holding your breath for a few seconds and then releasing. Repeat two or three times for maximum benefit.

One of the most powerful tools for healing and rejuvenating the body when it is in this relaxed state is to 'talk' to your cells to wake them up. Tell them off a little, as a parent might a child.

You can acknowledge your own slackness in not being vigilant enough and having allowed too much stress, but then just say something like, 'That is over now and it is time to function at my optimum level.' If this seems a little bizarre, just consider how often you have negative, worrying thoughts like, 'Oh hell, I look awful,' and are inwardly annoyed at your body for not firing on all cylinders.

Send love to your body cells. They are yours, intimately so – they *are* you. No one else owns them. They are your babies to nurture and also your loving structure, supporting and carrying you through life. They deserve the best you can give them.

Results

Almost right away your face will have a fuller, more integrated look, but it may take anything from ten days to a month or two before you realise that the lines and sagging skin have either disappeared or dramatically improved.

To achieve such results, the ideal would be to practise every day, but this is not practical for a lot of people. For a speedy change, however, it is a good idea to aim for three to four times per week.

Quite often when doing these exercises you will get a sudden hunch or inspiration to seek out something else that will help you – a new diet, a new book, a class. All these will help you achieve your perfect face and body.

The Last Word

Freedom from worry, stress and guilt allows your body to function as it was meant to. Gradually release all those ideas that leave you feeling confused, that immobilise you. Move through your day thinking, 'I am brilliant and beautiful.' Smile.

7

Take Control of Your Weight

'You are today where your thoughts have brought you;
you will be tomorrow where your thoughts take you'

James Allen

In this chapter, we are going to look at other formations on the lifeline that indicate worry and stress, paying particular attention to excess weight, which seems to bug quite a few of us.

Reading Your Hands

Islands or chained patterns appearing anywhere on the lifeline mean a period of difficulty that is bound to affect your health in some way, and which could affect your weight or the balance of foods you choose to eat. These difficulties usually revolve around relationship, money and/or work worries, and while you are putting these things right it's a good idea to keep a constant check on your health, including your weight if necessary. As you improve one area, the other will be enhanced as well.

Worry lines that move up from the lifeline towards the mount of Saturn (fig. 7.1) mean a time of restriction and enforced limitation. Astrologically, you are quite likely to have Saturn in an afflicted position in your horoscope at this time. However I have never known anything but good to come out of such patterns. The difficulties they represent appear to be a learning process, forcing you to

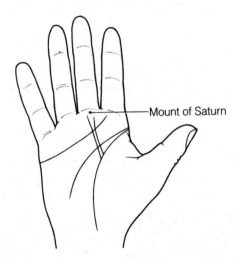

Mount of Saturn

look at yourself. In 90 per cent of cases, life takes on a whole new direction afterwards.

Sometimes these lines do not reach all the way to the mount of Saturn but stop at the head or heart line. If they end at the former it usually means some restriction around work; if the latter, it usually means the restriction is to do with your emotional life. If the line goes all the way up to the mount of Saturn, it means that the problem revolves around your whole approach to life.

People with soft, bloated hands often have a weight problem. They may not be very fat or necessarily much overweight, but they are retaining water in their tissues and therefore tend to gain weight easily. These kinds of hands often have a girdle of Venus located beneath the middle Saturn and Sun fingers (fig. 7.2), revealing a sensitive, supportive nature. Therein lies much of the problem.

The plus side is that you are aware, often acutely so, of the needs, pressures and/or expectations of people around

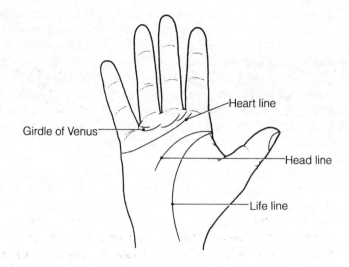

you. This can enhance your intuition and help you to see trouble or good things coming long before they happen. People with this sign are usually good at helping others.

The down side is that you can be oversensitive to the point of immobility. You can see what everyone wants and needs, and if these are in conflict with each other or with what you are doing, you just don't know what to do for the best. You are easily hurt and easily depressed.

Very creative people often have a girdle of Venus, as well as undefined boundaries, suggesting that other people can take advantage of them. They can become so involved with their own intuitive understanding of situations that they find it hard to switch off. If this sign is coupled with a head line that slopes steeply across the palm towards the mount of Moon, this person is not only deeply intuitive and imaginative but can be quite neurotic as well, with a tendency to retain fluid in their cells, leading to fluctuations in weight. Retained fluid is retained emotion, and in women this is reinforced by their hormonal cycle. Once life starts to flow smoothly, the water flows smoothly out of the system.

What tends to happen with sensitive people is that they become easily upset and release a lot of toxic chemicals into their system, perhaps from distress or confusion. The body signals overload and the body tries to stop the poisoning by encapsulating the toxins in water and fat.

Any sign on the hands that indicates stress can indicate a time of weight imbalance, whether the problem is gaining or losing weight. Weight can also come on and off as a result of love problems. On top of all this, our obsession as a culture with weight gain has led to a distortion in our thinking. What we need to do is to regain a balanced attitude towards weight and food – essential steps for gaining control of our bodies.

Excess Weight – An Attitude Problem?

The idea of being overweight is a peculiarly modern and Western phenomenon. In many other cultures a good covering of fat is a sign of health and prosperity. In fact, even in Europe before the First World War, when levels of infant mortality were high, families who tended to put on weight were regarded as the healthy ones with a greater chance of survival.

As we approach the millennium, with our health prospects at an all-time high and a vast choice of foods from anywhere in the world, we have become paranoid about weight and size. The fashion industry encourages a kind of masochism in us, whilst at the same time the latest research is coming full circle and telling us what our grandparents already knew: that a certain amount of fat is good for our long-term health.

So what should you do?

The answer is to keep an eye on current research, which is usually chronicled in an accessible way in the newspapers and magazines, and to begin to listen to yourself and your own body.

At first, listening to your own feelings about food is probably going to unbalance you a little. We all tend to want an authority to tell us what to do, because left to our own devices we are likely to stuff ourselves on the 'wrong' foods, or starve ourselves for fear of putting on weight. In fact, there are no really 'wrong' foods, only wrong attitudes, and the exercises that follow will help you to unravel some of these, leading you to a healthier, happier eating pattern that allows your weight to normalise itself. As you begin to get back into control of your body, your lifeline will begin to strengthen, exerting a positive influence over other difficulties in the rest of your life.

Unravel your feelings about food

Take a large piece of paper, turn it horizontally and draw a line down the middle.

On the left-hand side write down all your feelings about your weight, body size and food. Try to dredge up all those ideas that came from childhood, from school and your parents.

On the right-hand side write a positive affirmation to correct it. For example:

My mother is overweight and I'll end up like her	I am not my mother. My body follows its own rules, not hers
Cream cakes are fattening and I mustn't eat them	Cream cakes are delicious and I can eat them without getting fat
I must eat up all my food because of the starving people in Africa	I can leave my food if I want to. Eating it all up helps no one, least of all me
I've had a fat stomach for too long. I'll never get rid of it	The future is not the same as the past. My stomach is becoming flat and sleek right now

I can only lose weight by dieting. Crash diets are bad for your health, so if I lose weight, I could be ill

I do not need crash diets to lose weight. My body knows what to do and is reducing to my ideal weight right now

I hate cooking for the family. I'm sick of eating kids' food

Preparing food preserves life. I love my family and respect my role as life preserver – I don't have to eat what the kids eat. I can choose luscious foods just for me

Dieting is boring. I never succeed, so I'll always be overweight

don't need diets to lose weight. My body knows how to reach its best weight for health and vitality

Doing this exercise will show you some of your habitual thoughts about your body image and food even if you are basically a normal weight. It helps to get at the root of some of our other problems, particularly in the areas of love and family.

Make affirmations

Choose two or three of the affirmations from your list and write them out ten times, noting any resistance, which you should incorporate at the bottom. Remember to insert your first name after the word 'I'.

More affirmations

1. My stomach is smooth and flat and I have beautiful hips and thighs (put any part of your body you would like to improve)
2. I—am beautiful
3. I—am not my mother/father. My body responds to me, not her/him.

4. Cakes are delicious and I give myself permission to eat them when I want without putting on weight
5. I don't have to deny myself to lose weight
6. I give myself permission to eat spaghetti Bolognese (or whatever your favourite food is) when I want to without getting fat
7. Every day my body knows exactly what to do to create perfect health and my ideal weight

Are you getting some inner satisfaction from being overweight?

With the proliferation of slimming clubs and magazines, it is easy to believe that weight gain is purely scientific, that excess weight is simply the result of consuming too many calories for energy expended.

However, I have seen countless people where this equation does not add up. They can practically starve themselves and not lose weight, but as soon as their lives begin to move in the directions they want, or as soon as they change their thoughts about food, the weight begins to drop off.

In such cases the excess weight has often been stuck emotion, and quite often these people have had a vested interest in keeping it there. Their problems have been diverse but have usually centred on resentment of someone or something, or have reflected anxiety about their sexuality. If they are fat they can stave off unwanted attention from the opposite sex. Linda's story will show you what I mean.

Linda's story

Although Linda loved her husband and four children dearly, she was beginning to feel that her life, with its regime of regular meals, shopping and housework, was a benign prison. She had no life of her own, having happily given up working as a telephonist when she had her first child. She had never planned a career because she had expected domesticity to fulfil her. However, she was beginning to feel that her life was already over and the weight was starting to creep on.

Linda found that although writing affirmations helped, she got 'stuck' after a couple of weeks, feeling angry and resentful. The way she shifted this was to write out what was making her angry.

She wrote at length about her feelings and realised that her weight was a kind of self-punishment and something she could berate her family with. At a subtle level she was saying: 'Look how fat I've become caring for you lot. All I ever do is shop, prepare food, and clean up after you until four hours later when it all starts again.' Her weight was a visible symbol of her drudgery, but of course her family couldn't see the equation at all. They just saw a slightly overweight, rather cheesed-off Mum.

Linda solved the problem in the following way.

First of all, she wrote down:

- What subconscious satisfaction her weight was giving her
- Affirmations and actions to correct this

The first list looked like this:

1. I can blame my family for looking a drudge
2. My fat means I can be angry at everyone for trying to make me into a servant
3. My fat means I can feal sorry for myself
4. My fat means I can hate myself and feel helpless so I don't have to upset the family by doing what I really want to do (I really want to be joyous and lovely again with fashionable clothes and a fun lifestyle)
5. My fat is my weapon against the injustices and boredom of it all

Her second list contained these positive statements:

1. I, Linda, no longer need fat. I am beginning to feel gorgeous and life is opening up
2. I, Linda, no longer need anger. I chose to turn

myself into a servant and I now choose to open
my life into new, fulfilling directions

3. I, Linda, no longer need to feel sorry for myself.
It is my life and I can do what I like with it

4. I, Linda, release all my hate and resentment. I have
made a commitment to my family but I can also
begin to have the lifestyle I truly want

5. I, Linda, thank my body/myself for producing
such a potent weapon for me. I and my body
are all-powerful and we can now create a beautiful
body suitable for the lifestyle I really want

The positive actions Linda put on her list were things
that she truly wanted in her life, including some things
she could start straight away. One of these was joining
a swimming class, because she had never been able to
swim properly and was afraid of deep water; another was
to start learning the guitar as she loved guitar music.

The first time Linda learnt to dive – and diving had
terrified her since the age of three, when she had fallen
into deep water – she was so exhilarated that she glowed.
She lost four pounds overnight and continued to lose
weight every time she went to the class. Part of her
weight problem had been 'stuck' fear, and the class was
helping her to overcome this, not only her fear of water
but her fear of upsetting and losing her family.

In the guitar class, Linda made several new friends,
one of whom had a villa in southern Spain. Linda was
offered a free holiday for herself and her family and later
spent time there on her own with her new friend, which
helped to build up her own identity again. Today, Linda
has no weight problem and has a part-time job in a fashion
boutique.

Release your energy and your weight

If you have a weight problem, however small or large,
just take a few minutes to see what subconscious rewards
you get from being overweight. Doubtless, you will find

some and once you know what they are, you can deal with them.

Step 1   Write a list of any payoffs for being over-weight.

Step 2   Write a list of affirmations to correct them and, if necessary, any physical actions that seem appropriate.

Step 3   Practise the following technique for releasing stuck energy and weight to speed you towards your goal. You may find it easier to record it onto a tape and use the pause button as you need to.

Sit somewhere comfortably, relax and close your eyes. Breathe steadily and rhythmically, pretending that you are smelling a flower as you inhale and then letting your breath out like a sigh. Be aware of the breath as it moves in and out of your body and of the rise and fall of your diaphragm. Relax as much as your body wants to at this time.

Now take your awareness to the outlines of your body. Be aware of your feelings about your shape and your weight. Are there any parts of you that you feel miserable about?

How did those last few pounds get there? Did you stuff yourself? If so, why? Or did they go on even though you weren't eating very much? In either case, ask yourself what your feelings were just prior to the weight gain. You almost certainly weren't blissfully happy.

Were you hurt, upset, angry at someone?

Were you simmering with resentment?

Were you stuck in a situation over which you had no control?

What were your feelings? Really try to peel back the memories until you reach them.

Who are you angry at?

What are you resentful of?

Who isn't listening to you?

What is stopping you getting what you want?

Keep breathing deeply and feel those feelings. Breathe

and feel the distress like a bright spark of energy. Breathe into it.

Can you feel it in your body?

If you are really upset you may want to cry or to shout the things you couldn't say at the time. Take a pillow and yell into it if you want to. Turn it over and punch it, imagining the person or situation that has upset you.

You can take the process further back to key moments when your weight seemed out of control.

Repeat the process to get into your anger or distress or boredom and sift through the feelings until they become alive once more, released from their inertia in your fat cells.

When you feel you have done enough, rest quietly for a while and then bring yourself back to earth with a warm drink. If you have a friend or partner who will bring you one without thinking that he or she is involved with a nutter, so much the better.

I have known people lose a couple of pounds after one session using this process and just eating normally, but in a workshop situation lasting several days, I have known people lose quite a lot of weight and look years younger. The reason is that not only does the process work, but it begins to nurture you at a root level in your psyche so that different areas are healed at the same time.

Overhaul your body

Whilst all the above techniques are brilliant for getting you where you want to be, you may like a physical approach as well, a kick-start to get you going.

There are many excellent books on food and health, but the following simple regime is a particular favourite of mine. It can help you to cleanse your system, and possibly lose a pound or two, reinforcing any of the other exercises you choose to do.

If you are in any doubt about the advisability of such a regime, consult your doctor.

Breakfast   Fruit (any kind you find delicious and a treat), live, natural yogurt (I like the mild bio yogurt best) sweetened, if you like, with honey and/or fresh fruit.

Lunch   A large green salad composed of any vegetables and salad greens you love, accompanied by a protein. For example, you could choose from:
   Chicken
   Turkey
   Tuna
   Sardines
   Prawns
   Steak
   Cottage Cheese
   Eggs
Go easy on the salad dressing. Choose a high-quality one that isn't full of additives. If you are watching your weight, choose one that is fat free.

Dinner   *Either* a salad as above but with a different protein accompaniment plus a small slice of wholemeal bread; *or*, if you are not interested in weight loss, boiled pasta (preferably wholemeal, but it's not essential) or a baked potato. For an accompanying sauce make a ratatouille from onions, garlic, courgettes, aubergines stir-fried in a small amount of virgin olive oil. Add a small can of chopped tomatoes and generous amounts of herbs such as basil, oregano, mixed herbs and seasoning (but go easy on the salt). Ring the changes by turning the ratatouille into a chilli, adding beans and chilli.

   Although a purification diet is supposed to exclude tea and coffee, if you can't bear the thought of living completely without them, it's better if you include them, but don't drink so much and drink plenty of mineral water to flush out the system. You should try to drink six to eight glasses of water a day anyway.

   After three or four days on this you may be sick and tired of the sameness of it, so just stop and promise yourself that you can do it again when you want to.

   What you will achieve on these few days is a cleansing

of the liver, a clearer skin, brighter eyes, a lessening of the dark rings under the eyes, the loss of one or two pounds (more if you are quite overweight), a boost to your immune system and an antioxidant kick for your whole body. If you really want to give your body a kick-start, you can have the occasional day eating just fruit and drinking mineral water. I find that by the evening I'm nearly climbing the wall and I almost always cheat, but several spartan friends swear by it as a way of cleansing the body of toxins.

Give yourself a treat

After a few days on a restricted diet it's a good idea to give your body some of the foods it craves. This will help you to integrate some of the ideas around food that came up in your affirmations. Furthermore, if you have been denying yourself certain foods for fear of becoming fat, it will help to defuse the tension and lead you back to a more balanced eating pattern.

One of the great problems with dieting is that it tends to turn food into an enemy. This process helps you not only to make food your friend, but also to love your body.

Go to a store that stocks a wide variety of foods or to a specialist store that stocks the foods you know you want.

Let's suppose that you choose to go to a large supermarket.

You must go to this shop with the express intention of buying something special for yourself. Nothing else. No family shopping; no purchases for a cosy dinner for two. Nothing for anyone else at all. Only something for a delicious treat for you.

Enter the shop as you might a temple, full of reverence for the lovely nourishment you are going to give your most precious possession: your body.

Stand somewhere in the store and ask yourself what you would really love to eat. If you have been into denial for a long time you may feel stuck and no answers will come.

Now is the time to give yourself permission to have exactly what you long to eat.

Is it cream cakes?

Is it chocolate?

Is it piles of seafood?

Whatever it is, go and buy it.

Take it home or to a place that pleases you and begin to eat it. Enjoy every mouthful. Eat as much of it as you want, and then stop.

Don't go round thinking, 'I've just eaten five bars of chocolate. That's imbalanced, so I'd better have a "proper" meal.' Stick with what you've just eaten. Let it be your meal, and be aware of how you feel:

- Comfortable?
- Relaxed?
- Full?
- Bloated?

Don't judge the feeling. Just get on with your day or evening as normal until the next mealtime.

I've done this exercise many times. The first few times I wanted to feast on cream cakes because with everyone telling me that they would make me fat, I'd always tended to deny myself the pleasure of them. So, I'd stand there looking at the boxes of chocolate éclairs and cream meringues, knowing with total certainty that they were what I wanted to eat, but my conditioning against greed told me to buy just one meringue, one éclair.

However, my body was screaming, 'Take as many as you want,' so I did, and drooled on every mouthful. The first time, I consumed about 1,500 calories. I ate them for 'lunch' and my total calorie consumption for that day came to around 2,700, which is over the top for me.

On the scales the next day I was one kilo lighter.

The reason: I had enjoyed my food so much that my body had just shivered with delight. It had made me feel alive and in control. My body was being honoured and given what it wanted so it just processed the food normally to bring me closer to my ideal weight.

Nevertheless, within about half an hour of eating the cakes, I would also become aware of an unpleasant tingling in my head. The more I did this exercise, the more I felt alive because I was doing what I wanted, but my body was telling me very strongly that it didn't like the sensation of so much sugar. It wasn't long before I was balancing the two; giving myself pleasure from food without overdoing it.

It is the same when I go to France, which I do quite a lot because I love it. The food is so wonderful that I eat like a horse, savouring every minute and every mouthful. I usually come back home lighter than when I went, and there is an important health point here.

The French love their food and spend plenty of time enjoying it with family and friends. The latest research from the World Health Organisation states that statistically the French enjoy a level of immunity to heart attacks and other causes of premature death unmatched in the Western world. Other statistics support this and I firmly believe it is because they love and respect their food and eat what they want. They also drink wine in moderation and always have water and bread with their main meals.

Trust yourself

It is the same for all of us. If we love what we eat, we become more alive, but I mean love in the sense of honouring the body and not getting into a cycle of self-hate and denial if we are a bit overweight.

By eating the foods that call to us, sing to us, we are nurturing ourselves.

What you are doing is taking over control of your own eating patterns. Not all diets are suitable for everyone and some, such as low-fat diets, are being shown by researchers to be ignoring other physical needs such as the maintenance of bone mass, thereby causing further problems.

Your body knows what it needs. If you overdo things,

you will feel bloated and uncomfortable. If you starve yourself, you will feel empty and weak. The techniques above will begin to teach you to trust yourself.

If you still don't believe that your body really knows how to look after itself, perhaps the results of a research project carried out a few years ago will convince you. It was conducted on infants who had been eating solid food for a few months, so they were all around twelve to eighteen months old.

The children were offered a wide variety of foods and liquids and no attempt was made to encourage one kind over another. Although there was a wide diversity of choices made by the infants, some eating almost exclusively milk products, some mostly cereals and proteins, and so on, over the fortnight of the project each infant was shown to have balanced its diet perfectly with all the vitamins, proteins, carbohydrates and fats that it needed for development and growth. Not one of them overate.

What we as adults now have to do is recapture that instinctive knowledge and trust our bodies to get it right.

You can take the idea of treating yourself in order to learn about food and nurturing still further by spending a whole day eating only what you truly want. There are to be no shoulds and should nots. What you really must do is, though, check your inner feelings to see what you want. It is rare for a body intent on feeling good to say that it wants a whole packet of chocolate digestives followed by fish and chips and then half a chocolate gâteau all at one sitting. If it does, there is probably some other compulsion at work and now is a good time to discover what it is. Use the technique for releasing stuck energy and weight (see p. 144).

Anyway, let's just suppose that your eating habits are normal, if a little bit slapdash because of pressure, work, etc. The aim of this exercise is to release some of your blocks and to make you more aware of food.

When you wake up in the morning, what do you really

want? A cup of the strongest blast of caffeine you can find? Something fairly light like toast, a croissant or cereal, or the whole shebang of fried eggs, bacon, mushrooms and sausages? Whatever it is, *have it*. Give yourself permission to enjoy it.

When you have eaten it, be aware of how you feel. Heavy? Full? Light? Energised? Just be aware and accept the feeling. Above all, don't eat again until your stomach signals that it is empty.

This can be difficult if you are at work, so either do this exercise on a day when you are free or have your breakfast earlier – about five hours before lunch.

If you decide to go to a restaurant for lunch, choose exactly what pleases you and if you are working on prosperity as well, use the ambience to encourage feelings of wellbeing and wealth and don't get hooked up on how much it is costing. If possible, choose your meal without looking at the price. This is a huge signal to your subconscious that you are intent on having exactly what you want, that you are prosperous enough to go for it, and it will deliver results not only much quicker but often in quite surprising ways.

Do the same thing for your evening meal. Eat exactly what you want. If you have eaten fully at lunch, the chances are that you will only want something light, but let it be something that you love.

If you are doing this exercise properly and really letting your body be in charge, you will feel good. You will feel more in control of your life and it will have a knock-on effect in other areas like creativity, prosperity and relationships.

Take things gradually

Above all, you should take everything slowly and easily. Enjoy your food and enjoy your life. As you begin to enjoy your body as it moves towards its perfect state, you will achieve your results steadily without worrying about the speed of it all.

Your body knows how to get it right, but if you have setbacks, as we all do, just be easy on yourself and take it in your stride. After a holiday, for example, or Christmas, it is common for many of us to gain a few pounds. What is important is to enjoy yourself. After a while, as inner mastery is achieved, your weight will fluctuate less and less.

Even if it takes you several years to get what you want, it doesn't matter. You are going to be on the planet for a long time, so take it all gradually, have a good time and enjoy your body. It is the most brilliant machine you will ever use.

The Last Word

Have you ever stopped to think how superb your body is? All that bone, muscle, blood and flesh working away apparently by itself. In fact, your mind is in control, so begin to trust yourself and know that you can unravel problems and function at an optimum, super-level of health.

8

Take Control of Your Work Life

'What you can do, or dream you can, begin it. Boldness
has genius, power and magic in it'

Goethe

An old boyfriend once said to me, 'I can pinpoint the
exact moment when I became an adult: it was the moment
when I realised that I'd have to spend the rest of my life
working.' Another male friend, who dropped out and
hiked off to Nepal, said that part of the reason he had
done it was because there had to be something better
than a life spent working and supporting a family. For
both these men, the prospect of work filled them with
gloom; the way opportunities and career structures were
presented made them seem like servitude.

It is only in the past twenty years or so that women
have begun seriously to look for fulfilment in work,
and for many of them their level of satisfaction or
dissatisfaction has been obscured by their need to stake
a claim in organisations hitherto open only to men.

For both men and women the problems of maintaining
a secure foothold on the career ladder have led to their
abandoning other possibilities – maybe a year or two
doing something completely different, a year or two at
home with the children.

In our Western culture, this failure to pursue alternatives
has tended to lead to a narrowing of creative expression
in order to cater for a mass market. On a personal level,
pure creative expression either dies or is diverted to pay,

for example, for crippling mortgages lasting at least twenty-five years, or to satisfy the ferocious demands of children fed on a daily diet of advertising hype.

Indeed, so deep-rooted is this inertia that many people have chosen to suppress the fact that they have a highly individual spark which could make a unique contribution to society and maybe even help to improve it.

In fact, each generation has the opportunity to begin to do things differently. None of us is obliged to join the old structures if these are no longer serving us. We can begin to create new ones that support our new vision. Even if you are working in a corporate structure and are enjoying opportunities for rising up through the hierarchy, you still need to apply your creativity to see if those structures are organised for optimum success and fulfilment, and to use your creative energy to begin to change them if appropriate. The world is the way it is because human beings have organised it like this and each one of us is making a contribution to it, either actively by getting out there and adding to it, or passively by sitting back and

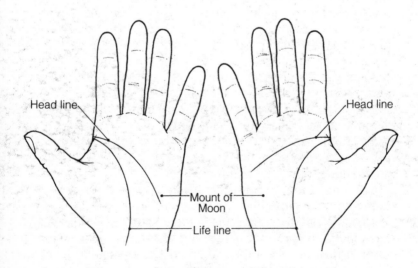

letting things happen.

This chapter will help you to recognise your unique talents and show you how to develop your potential to the full.

Reading Your Hands

There is one problem I have found over and over again on the head line: a gloriously creative left hand and a comparatively dull, pedestrian right one.

In figure 8.1 the head line on the left hand is sloping down towards the mount of Moon, indicating a well-developed intuition and creativity. On the right, it is moving straight across the palm, parallel with the bracelets of the wrist.

People with this pattern are naturally creative. They are dreamers and inventors and can come up with new ways of doing or looking at things. However, the right hand shows that although they have a good brain, they haven't done

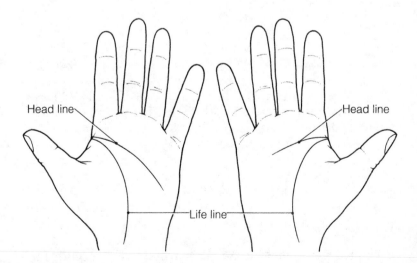

anything with their latent talents. They have opted for the easy way out, for security, for the obvious, and the world is a poorer place for it.

A head line that is clear and straight with a gentle slope is often found on the hands of professional people or executives, and because our society has so many outlets for people with this kind of flair I have not seen quite so many of them with problem hands. Where they *do* occur is when someone has natural business or professional acumen but has either chosen not to use it or has been prevented from using it for fear of the risks involved. In figure 8.2, for example, the left hand has a healthy, gentle slope that reaches right across the palm. The right hand is weaker and shorter, indicating a stunted development of talent.

The sign of creativity together with creative business acumen is a head line that forks.

In figure 8.3, the lower branch is heading for the mount of Moon, indicating imagination, intuition and ideas; the higher branch represents practicality and the fact that these ideas are being brought into the world. There is a free flow between the imagination and everyday life.

Often, however, the difference between the left and right hands shows that these factors are being thwarted.

In figure 8.4 the left hand shows a person who has all the qualities of someone who would be good in business, either a business of his or her own or at a high level in someone else's. However, the right head line is shorter and straight, indicating that this person has not fulfilled his or her potential and will almost certainly be feeling that something is missing in life.

The pattern in figure 8.5 is one I have seen a great deal and it denotes both courage and determination.

People with this weren't born with everything on their side. The foreshortened head line on the left hand shows that in some way their background was not conducive to business success, but by sheer hard work and holding on to their dream they have created all the elements of success in their lives. This pattern also occurs for

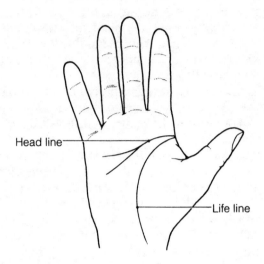

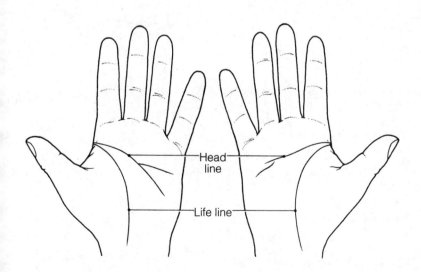

people who have not made the most of their educational opportunities. I have even seen university graduates with this pattern. They have gone through the motions of the educational system without any clear idea of where they are going, but some later trigger has brought out their latent talents and the right-hand head line has developed its longer slope and fork.

If your head lines are straight and you have a yearning to be your own boss, the very process of working towards your goal will create new lines that will show you are now following the right path in life.

A head line that is short but very strong and clear (fig. 8.6) shows someone who is capable of deep concentration, especially in a narrow field. Someone whose hands both have shortish, pale and rather weak head lines (fig. 8.7) has probably not set any great store by major achievement.

But it is very important to note that many people are happy with a life lived out of the high-flying league. The essential thing is that if you are happy with your work and lifestyle, then that is your purpose for the time being.

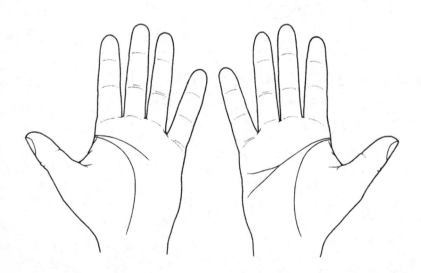

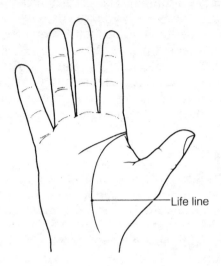

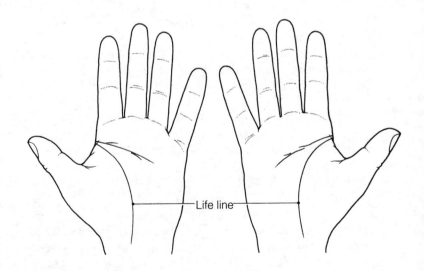

If you are not – and the discrepancies between your right and left hands will reveal this – then you will feel increasingly unfulfilled. The neural pathways in your brain are creating the lines on your hands.

If your head line on your left hand is strong and clear, but on the right is weak or short, islanded or feathery, you are going to feel a certain amount of frustration at some point in your life. This frustration is a healthy signal from the subconscious, warning you that something is wrong. It is trying to tell you to do something about it.

Roz's story

Roz had rather foreshortened head lines on both hands when I first met her about ten years ago. She was in her early twenties, with two small children and a husband who had his own successful small business.

She was completely happy. She lived in a comfortable, detached house which she had furnished and decorated luxuriously. She had an au pair to help her with the children and spent her days making sure that the house was immaculate before she went out to lunch with friends or up to London to shop or visit the theatre.

On both her hands, Roz's lifeline in her late twenties had an enormous break in it which, after a few fragile bridging lines, was taken up by the fate line. This meant a huge trauma and possibly the end of her marriage. Without spelling out the worst of what I could see, I did suggest that there could be a period of uncertainty ahead and encouraged her to think about a career for herself, and perhaps to take a look at her husband's lifestyle and legal affairs. She would not listen. She was happy and chose to live for the day.

The end came suddenly and tragically when her husband was killed in a car accident. Because he was so young he had not made a will and had no insurance. He died intestate with the house in his name. This meant that Roz received reasonable provision but the rest of his estate was divided up amongst Roz's children and other family members.

Because their house was part of his estate, she felt that she had to sell it and move into something smaller and cheaper to meet his obligations and the requirements of the intestacy.

She was in despair for about two years and took several cleaning jobs to keep her occupied and to bring in some money. During this time, the head line on her right hand began to grow longer and fork downwards, meaning that despite her natural disposition for a simple life, she was going to move towards a business career.

I gave her the techniques I am giving you and today she runs her own cleaning business with two vans and a team of 'blitz' cleaners who are contracted to offices and private houses.

Roz has bought another lovely home and works three days a week. The rest of the time she spends with her children, meeting her friends for lunch and going up to London as before.

She has often asked me if her husband's accident could have been prevented. At a party once he had briefly and very sceptically shown me his hands, which had revealed an enormous break on the left hand but just a weakness on the right. The only way he could have avoided that destructive break would have been to change his love of speed and drinking. (The night of the accident, his blood/alcohol ratio had been way over the limit.) In other words, he had a self-destructive quality in his make-up and he knew it. He said that if he couldn't get plastered after a hard week's work there was no point in living.

Roz had the traumatic line on her own hand because she was married to him and she had attracted him because in her late teens she had been pretty wild too. Only a change in lifestyle could have altered the pattern, and neither of them had been prepared to do it, despite the warning signs on their hands.

Of course, Roz's example is an extreme one in all sorts of ways. What it does show, though, and this is important for all of us, is how we need to recognise signs that tell us we need to change our direction in life, break down the barriers that are holding us back, if we are to find fulfilment. The rest of this chapter will show you how.

Discovering Your Own Dream

Each of us has a particular energy force to express, a special something to achieve in life that is unique to us. Often, however, this is thwarted by our environment or by the people around us until we are not sure in what direction we are really meant to be going.

Some of us are blessed with a very clear vision of what we want to achieve, but there are also many of us who have only a few vague ideas of what we think we want. We see the way other people live and think that we would like that too. Similarly, we see films and plays on television where people are in particular jobs, and certain things appeal to us.

This is all well and good, and indeed some people have discovered their true path by following up ideas stimulated like this, but it is very hit and miss and is not the best way to contact who you really are and do what is most fulfilling for you.

The following exercise will help you to discover your own ideal occupation. Even if you feel that you are already fulfilled in your work, doing this exercise may still uncover something that will add to your working life.

Everyone knows that every hand print is different – that is how forensic scientists work. Each of us is completely unique and different, and to get our life force flowing clearly, to get your life- and head lines vigorous and healthy, we have to contact a deeper level in yourself beyond your normal daily awareness. That level is the alpha brain-wave pattern which is described fully in Chapter 5. The following exercise uses that level to uncover your deeper energies and thereby your real dreams for what you want to do with your life.

Step 1   Make sure that you will be undisturbed for about fifteen minutes. To get yourself into a very relaxed state, use the technique described on pp. 100–102. If you don't have time for this, just breathe in an easy and relaxed way for a few minutes and then count slowly back from ten to one, relaxing more fully at each count.

With your eyes closed let thoughts come and go as they want. If you spend the first five minutes thinking about something else like what you're going to have for dinner tonight, that's OK. This is what is uppermost in your mind and if you are easy with it, or find you resolve some problem around it, it will eventually go away.

Step 2   When you have settled into this deepened state, let your mind wander to the thing that you would really like to do most. Forget your current occupation and let your thoughts drift into a place and position in which you would really like to see yourself, doing something you would really like to do.

At first nothing obvious may come to mind. You may just see yourself in pleasant surroundings – on a beach, at a concert, at a party, say. Let your mind play with these pictures. See what gives you pleasure, what activities spring to mind as being right for you.

- Do you see yourself on your own?
- Or are you in a crowd of people?
- Are you organising something?
- Or are you sitting down creating something?
- Perhaps you are taking a much-needed vacation?

Let your thoughts drift. See yourself moving in your mind's eye.

- Are you dressed in beautiful clothes?
- Evening dress perhaps?
- Or are you in jeans and tee-shirt?
- Are you in a luxurious environment?
- Or out in the open air?
- Are you by mountains, lakes, rivers?
- Or are you in a bustling town or city?

Let your mind free-associate as you see yourself in a situation that truly gives you pleasure, that makes you feel as you really want to feel with no hassles, no hang-ups, no problems.

Allow yourself as much time as you need for this. When you feel you have done enough, relax for a minute or two and then slowly open your eyes.

Whether you realise it or not, you have made contact with part of yourself that wants expression. The 'fantasy' you have just developed represents something you are meant to be pursuing. The images may be inexact and possibly even impractical, but the feeling behind them is real.

You may not feel that you want to act on them at this point, or, indeed, that there is anything *to* act on if your dreams seem really off the wall. But if you just rest easy with it, leave it for a day or two, or even, like some people, several months, you will start to feel a shift in the directions you want to take. Obviously, if you do this exercise several or even many times, your resolve and awareness will become stronger and your progress towards your goals much faster.

Jamie's story

Jamie was a dropout student working as a milkman while trying to develop a writing career and wondering what to do with his life. Each time he tried this exercise, he saw himself in smart hotels and restaurants dealing with beautiful things where he was the centre of attention. He saw himself greeting people in a holiday atmosphere of pleasure and fun. At first he thought that he just had a dropout mentality and tried to be more disciplined, but because the images were consistent, he decided to get a job in a smart hotel as a porter for a while. It was no worse than being a milkman and at least he would get to meet people.

While he was there Jamie noticed how many conferences and fairs were held in the hotel. He had always loved old paintings, so just for fun he decided to talk to the stallholders at the hotel's next antiques fair. Most of them told him that they were keen to find new venues, especially in new areas, and were kind enough to tell him what those areas were.

He did quite a lot of research into possible venues and the requirements for holding such fairs; and within a few months had found some hotels and halls in an under-represented region. He contacted the stallholders on his list, ran advertisements in the local press and on notice boards, and away he went, successfully and lucratively running antiques fairs and building up his expertise in fine art.

Edmund's story

In his visualising sessions, Edmund saw himself in narrow, confined streets. They seemed full of life and possibilities to him. He saw himself active amongst the greyness, the dirt. He saw money – lots of it – pouring out of dustbins and he saw himself walking amidst the litter dressed in a fine suit and expensive shoes.

The image amazed him because he was very New Age and into ecological issues, saving the planet, global warming, etc. Money was the last thing on his mind. He wanted political action.

He was working in a hospital at the time, doing mainly clerical work and studying counselling. After a few months he heard of a problem with waste disposal for patients with AIDS and hepatitis and decided to investigate. It was a very specialised field but he felt that he wanted to get involved. He applied for a job in a small private company that disposed of hospital waste and worked his way up from a clerk to a director.

I have included his story here because when I met him again very recently, he told me that he had effected a management buy-out. He is now chairman and managing director of the company.

Edmund still occasionally does 'finding your dream'

sessions. These are now leading him towards semi-retirement from the business and more into research into the spread of infectious diseases and the ecological issues concerning waste disposal.

By following his dream he has not only been able to make a considerable impact in his chosen field, but has also created a comfortable and fulfilling lifestyle for himself.

The Beginnings of Change

The point of the above stories is that Edmund and Jamie were not fulfilled and their lifelines were not as strong and clear as they should be during the first three decades of their span. However, once they had taken steps to look inside themselves to see the patterns they really wanted in their lives, they could then act on them and find fulfilment. Once they did, their lifelines began to show great energy and strength.

Make your ideas real

Now that you have some idea of the qualities that you want in your life, ideas that have come from your intuitive self (the right hemisphere of your brain), we are going to do some exercises which bridge it with the left hemisphere of your brain, i.e. your reasoning, practical self so that the two sides of your brain can begin to work together in harmony.

You will remember that the right hemisphere of the brain creates patterns on your left hand and the left hemisphere creates patterns on the right hand; so these two sets of exercises – the one you have just done, *Discovering Your Dream*, and the practical ones which follow – are designed to lift the blocks that are creating frustration between your true potential and what you are actually doing with your life.

Step 1   Take a piece of paper and at the top write:

In my ideal world my life would be . . . See yourself living in your ideal world and write down what your life would be like.

Step 2 Underneath this write: *In this ideal world my work would be . . .* What you write here may have similarities to your goal-setting from Chapters 1 and 2, but there may well be variations. Here you are sweeping away all barriers to possibilities in the area of your work. You are giving yourself carte blanche to see your work as you really feel you would like it to be and this often allows you to look at other areas of your life in unexpected ways.

For example, the first section on my list might look like this:

> *In my ideal world my life would be*: completely free of domestic chores. I would no longer be the skivvy and dogsbody. I would have charming, helpful children and family; freedom to travel with work when I want to or feel the need to get away; enough money not ever to worry about working at all, i.e. financial independence.

By doing this exercise I am showing myself how far away from the ideal my current life is. I need to sort out my domestic life and tighten everything up. My children think that going to school constitutes work and that nothing more is required of them. After doing this exercise, I make them understand that I have two jobs – work and looking after the house and them – and that I don't want to be constantly at risk of breaking my neck when I enter their rooms because their floors are knee-deep in clothes and books. This tightening up creates a lot more time for me. I get twice as much done and can take a week's holiday away from them. My ideal world is a few steps closer.

- If you have a partner and family your ideal world might bear some similarity to mine
- If you are single and living with your family or friends, you might want to create more space for yourself

- If you are living alone, you may want more company

Or perhaps your lists are revealing something altogether different?

The important thing is to act on them. It will be obvious how far away you are from your ideal. Take positive steps now to improve your life and work. Does your 'work' list contain a seemingly impossible dream? Something you would love to do but which seems light years away from your current life?

- Perhaps you are nearly sixty and would love to pilot an aeroplane?
- You are a clerk earning a minimum wage and would love to be working in television?
- You are a single mum doing a few cleaning jobs for petty cash but would love your life to open up to comfort, prosperity, or maybe glamour?

Your ideal work list will tell you what your real desires are, and now is the time to do something about them. It doesn't matter how small the steps are as long as you begin to take them. Fate is magnetic – whatever you do to honour your true self will attract more and more to you. Once you open up to yourself, the world will be on your side and you will no longer be buffeted about by other people. You will be free of those negative situations we all create for ourselves when we don't know what it is we want. You may find that your desires change as you move some of the old obstacles out of the way; your path will become clearer and easier as you see more precisely what it is you really want to do. First, though, here's how to overcome those obstacles.

Clear away the obstacles

This exercise will help you to overcome any obstacles in your life so that you can move towards your ideal. You may want to put it on tape or get a friend to read it to you.

Make sure that you have an uninterrupted fifteen minutes or so to sit or lie down for this process.

Follow the full relaxation exercise on pp. 100–102 or simply close your eyes and breathe rhythmically for a few minutes. Become aware of the passage of air through your nostrils into your lungs and the rise of your diaphragm, then its fall and the release of air back out through your nostrils.

Count slowly back from ten to one.

In this relaxed state imagine the obstacles in your life as a wall. You can see this wall in the distance. You are on a hill and as you look down on the wall, although it is high you can see over it. You do not see it as a problem.

As you begin to walk down the hill, however, the wall begins to look larger, and as you come right up to it you can see that it is thirty feet high and an impenetrable barrier. It contains all the blocks in your life, both past and present.

But look again. You have missed something. The wall is not solid. It is porous, with large man-size gaps in it. You slip through one of these and there, inside the wall, you can see all your problems. These problems are not the wall. The wall is porous. You can walk through it. The problems are like bits of litter, just a minor nuisance on your way.

Take a good look at them. See their shape. Do they have a colour? Is there anything else remarkable about them? Give yourself a minute or so to examine them.

These are your negative thoughts about your situation. You created these thoughts and you can destroy them.

Do that now. Destroy them. In any way you like.

Shoot them.

Dissolve them.

Get an army to surround and obliterate them.

Get a lion to devour them.

Use any image of destruction that seems final and complete.

The space inside the wall seems empty now. If it

doesn't and something still lurks, see yourself as strong and invincible and simply crush whatever remains.

Sometimes a shadow still lurks. Don't worry. You have done a great deal towards sorting out your ideas. Improvement is guaranteed and you can repeat the process whenever you like to complete the task.

As you look around the wall, you can see that it no longer has any substance. You can walk right through it to the other side.

This wall has been blocking your landscape for so long that you may have forgotten the dreams, ideas and plans you had, so walk through the wall now.

Make yourself walk right through the no-substance to the other side, where you will find those lost ideals.

See yourself surrounded by the life you really want. See yourself walking right up to a building where you are doing the job you have set your heart on, or the business you have secretly planned. See the people around admiring you. See your colleagues respecting you and giving you a pat on the back for your success. See your customers or clients queuing up for your goods or services. See them discussing how brilliant you are.

Populate your landscape with loving, supportive people; paint it in lush colours, and give it scenery that encourages in you a feeling of wellbeing, prosperity and fulfilment.

You can repeat this technique as often as you like. You will notice a difference right away, and although the speed with which results occur varies from person to person, your life *will* begin to change for the better.

Making Change Happen

Let us suppose that, like most of us at one time or another, you are at a crossroads and want to change your job or even your career. If you are single with no obligations it is perhaps easier, but for many people the risk of making a mistake and losing everything is often too great.

There are two ways to approach this problem:

- The intuitive, right-brained way (creating patterns on your left hand)
- The practical, left-brained way (creating patterns on your right hand)

The intuitive, right-brained approach

For this you have to trust that your intuition is right. Once you are familiar with using it, it always is, but it can lead you into some seemingly scary situations.

To contact your intuition, I find it is best to lie down either on a sofa or on the floor. Breathe rhythmically for a few minutes and then count slowly down from ten to one. When you feel peaceful and fairly floppy, take your awareness down to the gut area of your body, the navel or *hara*. According to the Japanese tradition the *hara* is where your life force resides.

Ask your intuition what you should be doing about your job. Should you change to something different? If so, what?

Just breathe easily and wait a few moments in a 'listening mode'. You may get an answer at this point, but don't worry if you don't.

Now, gently draw your awareness smoothly upwards over your solar plexus, heart and throat to your head, so that a link is formed between your intuition and your reason.

You may get an instantaneous flash of insight, or you may get a vague feeling.

Don't worry. An answer will come, either within hours or within a day or two. People usually find that they just naturally act in a different way; that they are suddenly positive about wanting to move on and find something else. There is rarely any doubt about the decision.

Samantha's story

Samantha was a massage therapist. She had been doing this for eight years and was deeply intuitive and knowledgeable, with a client list that was the envy of all her fellow practitioners, but she was getting tired of it. She decided that she had had enough, but with a mortgage, car and comfortable lifestyle she didn't fancy taking the plunge into anything else that would almost certainly pay less.

She did the above exercise, and because her distress with her work was so acute the answer shot up like a geyser: double your fee and halve your client list.

She emerged from the technique shaken and amazed. She was already charging a little above the going rate and the prospect of doubling it seemed obscene and basically immoral. She also believed that if people felt the need to see her, it was her duty to accommodate them somehow.

Because her logical left brain wouldn't let her go the whole hog, Sam compromised. She kept her favourite regulars at the old rate and told all newcomers the doubled fee.

She said that she nearly choked the first few times she quoted her new charge. Often the response was a gasp followed by polite refusal, but one or two people took her up, and then a few more.

They were rather different from the clients she had been seeing. Either they were comfortably off, or they believed in spending money on themselves. Either way, their energy was less draining than the others and Sam enjoyed seeing them much more.

Gradually, she did as her intuition had guided her and charged all her clients the new rate. Many of the old ones dropped away, with the result that her client list was halved.

The very month that she achieved what her intuition had told her – double the fees and half the number of clients – Richard came to see her. They became friends and then lovers. He was starting a therapy centre in Spain and asked her to join him, which she ultimately did. When she asked him how he had come to contact her in the first place, he said, 'Because you were no cheapskate. I thought that anyone who had enough self-esteem to charge such a huge fee for a massage had to be someone I wanted to meet.'

Today they are very prosperous and happy and charging the going rate for their work. Sam's intuition had simply guided her towards a more fulfilled life and tested her feelings about herself and money into the bargain.

The practical, left-brained approach

Although this is a logical approach, it also contacts your creative self. Both this and the previous exercise are designed to connect the two hemispheres of your brain.

Take a piece of paper and at the top write: *Fifteen things I could do to make a living* . . . Put the numbers one to fifteen down the margin and then write whatever comes into your head. It may seem absolute rubbish at first, but just keep at it, free-associating as you go.

If you don't stop to think, this technique by-passes your logical mind and will tap into some areas that have importance to you. There may be a pearl in your very first list, but don't worry if there isn't. Do the process once a day for a week or two and you will be surprised at the ideas that come up.

Other possible headings for this brainstorming approach are:

- Fifteen ways I could increase my income
- Fifteen things I love doing
- Fifteen things I love doing to make money
- Fifteen ways I could save money
- Fifteen different careers I could move into
- Fifteen ways of having a fabulous time
- Fifteen ways of making money by having a fabulous time
- Fifteen ways I could make money from my house
- Fifteen ways I could make money from my car
- Fifteen businesses I could open up
- Fifteen businesses that would make me fabulously wealthy

- Fifteen businesses that would make me happy
- Fifteen businesses that would make me happy and wealthy

It takes such a short time to do, so you could choose two or three. It seems like a silly game at first, rather like Consequences, but you will be surprised at how effective it is.

When you have done it for two or three days, see if there is anything you can act on.

Chris's story

Chris was in dire need of money. His wife had divorced him and kept the marital home, plus he had to provide maintenance for her and the children. He had a full-time job, but it left him with just enough money for his newspapers and a few drinks.

He tried this technique and his first attempts were full of criminal things like:

'Go round and murder ex-wife.'

'Rob a bank.'

'Steal ex-wife's car (since I'm paying for it).'

But a few pearls were also appearing, one of which was: 'Be a taxi driver.'

It was a joke, written off the top of his head, but as he looked at it he realised that it had possibilities. He knew someone who ran a taxi service where people used their own cars, so he decided to give it a whirl for a few hours each evening.

He was taken on and very quickly began to make more money than he had believed possible in the circumstances. He had been living in rented accommodation and within a fairly short space of time had enough for the deposit on a house.

But his wife found out, and as is often the case in acrimonious divorces, assumed that he had been lying to her about his financial status and began to demand more money.

Chris went back to the brainstorming techniques and did them many times more until he came up with a solution.

He threatened to take his ex-wife back to court, but managed to achieve an out-of-court settlement that gave them a clean break. He changed his job and moved to another part of the country so that he could make a fresh start. His children were well into their teens and therefore able to make their own choices about coming to see him, which reduced any further heartache.

Siobhan's story

Siobhan used a combination of both techniques.

Her life seemed an absolute shambles. She was bright but hadn't known what she wanted to do when she left school after her A-levels. She had dropped out for a while and gone to live with a casual boyfriend, but was now working at a supermarket on the checkout to earn enough money to keep her going for a while. In between shifts, she just read novels.

In an effort to help her get her life together a friend came with her to see me. She was clearly marking time and feeling at a dead end. Her left hand was brilliantly creative, with a steeply sloping head line that also forked. Her right head line was straight and weak.

I gave her all the goal-setting techniques in Chapter 2, plus the exercises in this chapter. Doing the 'unblocking' exercises (p. 166–170) made her see instantly that she had been running away in the belief that a creative life is impossible except for the super-lucky or super-gifted. At the same time, when she contacted her intuition it hit her like a bombshell that she wanted to have a business and be her own boss, but she did not want to belong to the commercial rat race. She would rather go back to dossing around with her boyfriend and working on Sainsbury's checkout than sell out.

At first, I encouraged Siobhan to think in terms of money creating freedom for her to do what she really wanted. Big mistake. She wanted an alternative society. Money was for the bare essentials only.

But I hadn't entirely lost her. She was hooked on these techniques and kept on using them, saying they were the best thing since sliced bread.

Her casual boyfriend became a permanent one. Once the commitment was made, he began to make plans for the future, getting himself a job on a motorway building site where he earned a great deal of money. When he had saved up £10,000, he and Siobhan packed up and left England for a remote area of France. For approximately £8,000 they bought an almost roofless 'farmhouse' with outbuildings and three acres of land. They then bought a goat and chickens, cultivated the land to become as self-sufficient as possible, and began rebuilding the house. Siobhan also started doing what her intuition had told her.

She fulfilled two aspects of her creativity by:

- Writing freelance articles and stories based on her experiences
- Creating the most exquisite quilts I have ever seen

She made dozens of these quilts for the sheer love of it, until, in order to make a bit more space, she exhibited some of them for sale. They were snapped up immediately and she was commissioned for a great deal of money to make more.

She was back up against that old devil, commercialism, and almost told her would-be clients no. However, her intuition told her to find a balance, so she now takes only those commissions she feels are right and knows that she will love.

The result: she takes a lot more commissions than her right brain would have planned, their home is exquisite, especially as the walls are festooned with her glorious quilts, they have no money worries, and they are very happy.

Siobhan's weak head line on her right hand has now strengthened up, but it still does not fully match her left one. She has noticed the change developing on her hand

and realises that she is still not fulfilling her potential. She feels this as a niggling doubt but has chosen, as her right hand shows, to stay as she is for the time being.

Your own head line and your work

Without even glancing at your hands you know how you feel about your work. If you are contented, your head lines will be more or less similar in length and slope. If you are frustrated in any way the lines will be different; and you can acknowledge it and begin to move towards the work you really want to do.

The Last Word

Imagination is the source of our creativity. In our imaginations we can achieve anything. But many of us stop there. From now on, let your imagination be the nursery of your life; let the ideas move out from your mind. Act on them. Make them real. Be what you dream to be.

9

Take Control of Your Self-Esteem

> "'Tigger is all right, really," said Piglet lazily.
> "Everybody is really," said Pooh. "That's what *I*
> think . . . '"
>
> *Winnie the Pooh*, A. A. Milne

Very few of us, even the most apparently confident, have
not, at some time or other, been exposed to the idea that
we are in some way lacking.

From infancy we pick up negative ideas that we don't
even remember as part of the process of being 'civilised'.
It's always:

'No.'
'Don't touch.'
'Naughty.'
'Dirty.'
'You'll fall.'
'You'll hurt yourself.'
'It's dangerous.'
'Be careful.'

Parents mean well – and I, as a parent, also meant
well when I said it to my own children – but the result
is that most of us grow up feeling somewhat fearful
and that the world out there is a dangerous place. Our
creativity, courage and self-expression are half stifled
before we begin.

In schools, too, in order to enhance the purest academic
development, our minds are moulded into intellectual

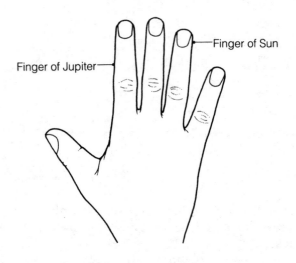

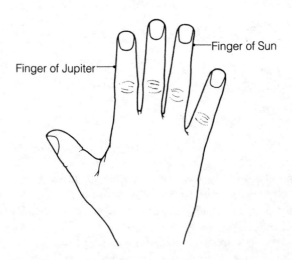

straitjackets. If you don't conform, you either fall by the wayside or become a maverick. Most of us pick up an unhealthy dose of anxiety about our abilities and seek approval from teachers who, by the nature of their work, do not usually have time to give us very much attention. None of this is good for encouraging self-esteem.

Reading Your Hands

Some people are naturally ambitious and determined, and either rise above or ride roughshod over the system.

Almost invariably, if you are one of these your finger of Jupiter (index finger) will be longer than your finger of Sun (3rd finger). See figure 9.1.

If this pattern appears on your left hand but on the right hand your fingers are either level or the finger of Jupiter is shorter than Sun (fig. 9.2), it means that your innate nature is ambitious but you have been thwarted or crushed by circumstance. It can also indicate that despite your desire for success, you lack the will, determination or organisation to achieve it in the way you want.

If the position is reversed, so that on your left hand your finger of Jupiter is shorter, but on your right hand it is longer than your finger of Sun (fig. 9.3), it means that by nature you are not ambitious but have been forced into it by circumstances. Although you will probably achieve good results, your heart won't be in it and you will always have a tendency to want to opt for a softer life.

Generally, a shorter finger of Jupiter in comparison with Sun means that you tend to consider the feelings of others (especially if you have a girdle of Venus; see Chapter 7), and other people can sometimes outmanoeuvre you leading to lower self-esteem. This often happens in the workplace. People you regard as good friends or colleagues can be quietly enhancing their careers at your expense, perhaps by doing extra work, perhaps by putting a few soft words in the right ear, perhaps by simple out-and-out jockeying for position. Those with

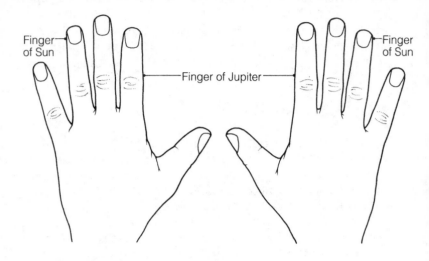

Finger of Sun — Finger of Jupiter — Finger of Sun

the less assertive, shorter Jupiter finger can feel hurt and misled, which only reinforces a low self-esteem.

Another major indication of the state of your confidence and self-esteem is the second (middle) phalange on your finger of Jupiter. If it is full and balanced with the other two phalanges, it means that you do believe in yourself and sooner or later you stand a good chance of getting what you want. If it is narrow or wasp-waisted in comparison with the other two phalanges (fig. 9.4), it means that you lack confidence.

The phalanges of the thumb show a similar picture. The three phalanges traditionally mean the will (the first phalange), ability/confidence (the second phalange) and the strength of desires or wishes (the mount of Venus, beneath the thumb). If the latter is fleshy, you have healthy appetites and a love of life, and if this is coupled with full first and second phalanges, it means that you have both the ability and the strength of will to achieve your aims. If any of these are thin-looking, your will and/or your confidence needs some help.

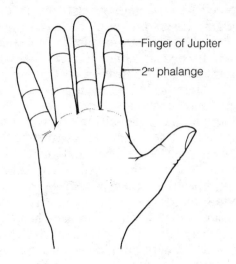

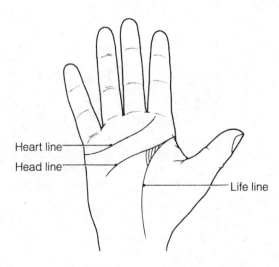

Another manifestation of blocked energy that invariably means considerable lack of self-esteem is a life- and head line joined at the beginning and then connected by a series of bridging lines to a length of two or more centimetres (fig. 9.5). This pattern means that the person is deeply attached to his/her childhood family, whether parents or guardian. The connecting or bridging lines usually represent attempts to become independent that have failed at some fundamental level.

Although the parental link may be a loving one, the bridging lines indicate a frustrated creativity or development that has been put on hold. It also often suggests a fear of the world beyond the home, which can cause health problems.

Quite often, though, this pattern is seen on one hand only. If on the left hand the life- and head lines are joined, but on the right they are separate (fig. 9.6), it means that this person was brought up in a cocooning or even restrictive household but has broken away and begun to develop his or her own life.

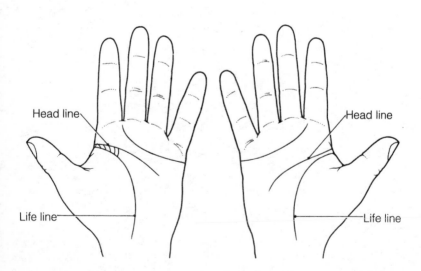

Head line · · · · Head line

Life line · · · · Life line

If the pattern is reversed, so that the lines are separate on the left hand but joined on the right, although the energy of this person is naturally free and expanding, it is being clamped in some way, either vigorously or subtly. This person will not be able to move forward properly until he or she has broken free of the restrictions of the family or childhood.

Mandy's story

Mandy's life- and head lines were joined on both hands. On her left the bridging lines reached up her lifeline to around the age of thirty; on her right to around the age of twenty-one. She has a powerful, successful father and a mother who devoted her life to her family and could not let go.

Mandy is bright and wanted to go to university. However, her father – a self-made man with little education – was opposed to her going, whilst her mother dreaded the idea of her daughter leaving home. As a result, Mandy remained at home and took a secretarial course at a local college, becoming more and more frustrated.

After she started work, she met and fell in love with a high-flying computer manager. They married when she was twenty-one, which was the point at which the family ties ended on her right hand. Within a few months he began working for an American company and shortly afterwards was sent to the States to work.

Mandy's mother was up in arms, trying to persuade her to stay in their home in England and becoming mysteriously ill with a nervous complaint. Mandy herself was distraught. Until now all her experience of life had been distilled through her mother. As a result she had lost her own sense of direction. She felt anxious and guilty and her parents made it clear that for her to go to the States would make her mother seriously ill.

Of course, Mandy's husband put his foot down, so Mandy went to the States and became ill herself with a bladder and kidney complaint. She couldn't shake it off and was in and out of hospital for two years, and on antibiotics and treatment for a further five. The marriage was in shreds, with Mandy longing to go home and be looked after by her mother.

However, they hung on together and when she was twenty-nine Mandy became pregnant. When the baby was born her mother flew over to be with her but barely acknowledged her new grandson. All she wanted to do was to talk to Mandy and try to coerce her into returning to England. This pattern continued after her mother's departure with telephone calls in which her mother would often forget even to ask about the baby.

Mandy was now thirty and adored her son. Her marriage was coming back together, her health was practically back to normal and she suddenly saw how dangerously manipulative her mother had been. This was the point on her left hand when the family bond was finally put into perspective.

Mandy is now thirty-five and has three more children. Her husband's career has brought them back to England again and her parents have settled into a much healthier relationship with her.

Mandy's is a classic case of an early family pattern working itself out to completion. But it could all have been improved and the suffering to Mandy's husband and her own health avoided.

The Beginnings of Change

We are all the products of our upbringing, for better or worse, and we all have family problems to work out, whether they are from sibling rivalry or parental relationships. Very often these are loving and good, but it is rare to find them completely trouble-free.

The first and most important thing is to honour yourself at all times. Most of us have loving parents trying to smooth our paths, but even when this is the case, we can feel guilty when we know that we want something of which they disapprove. I have seen middle-aged people and older racked with guilt because their parents are elderly and they themselves want to live abroad or do something that will take them away a lot.

The answer is to hold on to your dream no matter what the obstacles. Family difficulties will nearly always work themselves out for the best.

In the next exercise we are going to go back to that time in your life when a lot of these thought patterns began – your childhood. If you have no negative signs on your lifelines and forefinger you will probably still gain some benefit from the exercise because it will put you in touch with half-forgotten parts of your psyche that can be given a healing boost. Like most of the other exercises, this should be done when you have ten to fifteen minutes of peace and quiet. You may find it easier to make a tape and use the pause button as necessary.

Healing the wounded child

Sit or lie down comfortably. Relax and breathe gently, feeling the air moving in and out of your lungs. Relax each part of your body, moving up from your feet to your head.

Now take your thoughts back to when you were four or five and your first day at school. See the school building, the playground and all the other children. Hear the noise and feel the air against your face. See the clothes you are wearing, your socks and your shoes. Is your mother with you? Your father? Or is there someone else?

See yourself entering the school. What does it look like? What pictures are on the walls? What are the desks like?

Give yourself a minute or so to remember this:

- What does it smell like?
- Is there a lot of noise?
- What does your teacher look like?
- Where do you hang your coat?

Above all, how do you feel?

- Are you interested?
- Are you excited?
- Are you full of anticipation?
- Or are you terrified?
- Is the change too much to bear?

See yourself in your memory's eye and really remember the feeling, really see yourself as you were then.

Give yourself another minute or so to remember. Would you have liked things to be different?

- A different school?
- A different atmosphere?
- A different emotion in yourself?

Give yourself a few moments to see and feel this.

Now we are going to add something to the picture.

Imagine that you are the big person who brought you to school. Perhaps this was your mother, or maybe someone else. Bend down and look into the eyes of the child that is you and say:

'This is an important day for you. You are going to meet a lot of new people and do a lot of new things that you will enjoy. No matter what anyone says to you, never forget that you are as good as they are, and never forget how very special you are. There are things that you are going to do in the world that absolutely no one else can do in the way that you can. You are going to make new friends here and sometimes they may upset you, but nothing and no one can ever harm you unless you allow it. If you don't like any situation in life, you can change it. You can make your world any way you want it. Never ever forget that. You are in control of your life, no one else.'

Give the child that is you a hug and a kiss and send it off with confidence for its new venture.

Allow yourself a few minutes to settle. Perhaps you will recall some events or people from school very vividly. If the memory is a difficult one, allow yourself to re-experience it, but also make it clear to yourself that it is over. You are older and wiser now and you can loosen its hold over you. Mentally cut the ties that bind you to it. Take a pair of imaginary scissors to the memories and cut them clean away.

Now we are going to take a step further back. Take your thoughts back to the very first things you can remember.

You are a baby:

- Are you in a pram or cot?
- Is the radio/television on?
- Are you out in the open air?
- Is someone saying something to you?
- If so, what are they saying and doing?
- What are you thinking?
- What are you feeling?

These are some of the first conscious thoughts and decisions you made about yourself and your world, and if you don't think that they are serving you now, *you can change them right here*. You can begin to alter your basic programming.

Say to yourself: 'There are certain things I want to change. That particular situation is over and finished now and I release it.'

Perhaps the memory is a pleasant one. It is still important to tell yourself that that is all it is, a memory, and that you have complete control over any thoughts you have.

Now paint a picture in your mind's eye of your ideal childhood. Paint the room in the soft or vibrant colours you like. Hear the voices of the adults telling you how unique and wonderful you are. Forgive them for any harshness they may have expressed to you, any doubts.

See those doubts and that harshness as words and pictures on a blackboard.

Now take a cloth and wipe the board clean. The words and actions have gone, so let go of them yourself. See them attached to your body like bits of sticky tape. Pick the tape off now and burn it for the rubbish that it is.

Now try to make contact with the raw energy that was you as a tiny baby.

You have enormous resources and potential. There is nothing beyond you and your immediate awareness. You are a powerful human infant with no doubts about your force or intention. You have not heard anything negative because you cannot understand.

Start to imprint on your powerful infant self the ideas that you would have liked to grow up with.

You are lovable. You are delightful. The world is a better place for your arrival in it. You are going to grow up to do good and important things. You are going to grow up attracting love and friendship. Your life is useful and fulfilling.

Now slowly return your thoughts to your adult self and say inwardly that your life is improving dramatically from this moment on.

A personal story

My own first conscious memory was of being pushed in a pram up a busy street by my mother in the city where I was born. We went to the flat of a friend of hers who also had a child. As I played with the child I was aware of how dark and gloomy the flat was and how miserable and rasping my mother's friend was, how she kept telling me and her child not to do this, and not to do that.

As a mere baby I couldn't know what had made my mother's friend like that, but it was the beginning of a lifetime of wanting to create light and space around me, and also the beginning of a childhood dread of authority figures like my mother's friend. I was scared something awful would happen to me if I offended them, and because the nature of adults is to boss small children about, this first notion was often reinforced.

Of course, it wasn't only my mother's friend who created this situation. What she did was to burst into my consciousness with an idea and I hung every other similar example of adult behaviour on to this. Even to this day my nerves contract if someone is annoyed by something I have done, and there are quite a few of us who do the same or respond with anger. It is a cultural malaise – a malaise we can begin to heal.

Affirmations

From the muscle-testing exercise in Chapter 6 you will have seen how much your words can affect your body, so now try saying these affirmations out loud, inserting your first name after the initial 'I':

1. I—am a wonderful, perfect human being
2. I—now release all doubts about myself
3. No one in the world can ever be like me
4. I—am unique and superb
5. Other people respect me exactly as I am
6. I—forgive myself for dwelling on my doubts about myself
7. I—am beautiful/handsome and growing more attractive every day
8. The more I—let go of my old doubts and feelings, the more others see my true beauty and perfection
9. My body now shapes its contours according to the perfection in my mind's eye
10. I—now realise that I like myself
11. I—am my own best friend

It is possible that you may feel a little uncomfortable about these. That's absolutely fine. It means that you are beginning to shift your feelings and energy about yourself.

Perhaps you feel euphoric and 'Yippee, I'm a pretty marvellous person.' Excellent. You are really getting somewhere.

Now continue with the following exercise.

Mirror Work Go up to a mirror and look yourself straight in the eye. Gaze at your reflection as you would a beloved relative or friend you want to make feel good about his or herself and say: 'I really like you. I think you are wonderful.'

OK, try to stop laughing at the absurdity of it, or grimacing and saying, 'Oh God, I look terrible.' Your reaction shows just how little you rate yourself and how much you look for confirmation of your worth from other people. If you depend on other people to bolster your self-esteem, you are nearly always going to fall short because they probably don't feel 100 per cent sure of themselves either.

Now take the affirmations you have just spoken aloud and say them while you look yourself in the eye in the mirror.

Don't worry if you are still feeling uncomfortable. You are tapping into your deepest insecurities, those feelings that say you're a pathetic little nobody with less than perfect looks and body.

Now say these affirmations in the second person, as if you are a teacher, parent or friend talking to your reflection. Most of our negative ideas about ourselves come from other people saying you're this or you're that, so our psyches get so used to accepting information about ourselves in this way.

The affirmations will now look like this, with your first name now inserted after the first 'you':

1. You—are a wonderful, perfect human being
2. You—are releasing all doubts about yourself
3. No one in the world can ever be like you
4. You—are unique and superb
5. Other people respect you—exactly as you are
6. You—can forgive yourself for dwelling on your doubts about yourself
7. You—are beautiful/handsome and you are growing more attractive every day
8. The more you let go of your old doubts and feelings, the more others see your true beauty and perfection
9. Your body now shapes its contours according to the perfection in your mind's eye
10. You—now realise how much you like yourself
11. You—are your own best friend

Does that seem a bit easier than the first exercise? If so, it is because we find it hard to set ourselves up as something marvellous by ourselves, but if someone else tells us so, we tend to believe it.

If saying the affirmations this way appeals to you, you can turn all the affirmations for prosperity, love and work around the same way. They are *your* affirmations. It is your life and you can use them in whatever way pleases you.

Finally, look in the mirror and pretend you are a chat-show host or hostess giving a brief summary of who you are on television before introducing you to the audience. Say whatever pleases you and be as dotty and over the top as you like.

If you find that looking into a mirror and saying these things is a bit too much, you can get good results by closing your eyes and visualising the scene and mentally saying the words. The important thing is that in your mind you are putting yourself in the place occupied by the stars that tend to dominate our culture. You are saying that you are at the very top of the tree in our society, which is a big boost to your self-esteem.

You can change the words to suit your life as it is now, and also, from time to time, to help to bring in the things you want in the future.

I have seen some remarkable results produced by this technique, especially with young people whose careers have not yet properly started.

Becka's story

I first met Becka about eight years ago when she came to see me with her mother who didn't know how best to guide her. She was then aged seventeen and very confused. She was bright but didn't have a clue what she wanted to do. I gave her several techniques, but the one she liked best and used the most was the mirror technique.

Not only did her mother often overhear her talking into her mirror, but, with Becka's consent, she brought me a copy of one of her 'chat-show introductions'. Here is part of it:

'Good evening, ladies and gentlemen. Our special guest tonight is Becka, who is best known to you as chairman of the most successful banking house in Europe. Becka's strength has always been to save money and cut corners, starting when she was a little girl with her piggy bank and post-office savings account.

'Today, as we all know, Becka is world-famous for her business acumen, her beauty and charm. So popular that she is always out with admirers, she is nevertheless warm and caring and enjoys needlepoint.'

In fact, Becka was very shy and retiring and very mousy to look at. She carried herself as if she wanted to curl up into a ball. Her greatest pleasure was, indeed, saving money and spending small amounts of it on nail varnish – she had exquisite hands – rings and bracelets. It was as if she wanted to adorn the extremities of herself while ignoring her core.

Anyway, she got quite carried away with the mirror technique and when I saw her two years later I hardly recognised her. She was beautifully dressed and made-up, looking more like a model than a mouse.

She loved accounting and money but had decided against accountancy or banking because they were too dull and pedestrian for the image she now had of herself. Instead, she chose to study information technology and today has her own small company supplying specialist packages to industry and commerce all over Europe.

Her lifestyle is enviable, with an apartment in London and another in Switzerland that she shares with her Swiss boyfriend.

At the age of seventeen she looked as if she was destined for a life of back-room boredom. Her finger of Jupiter on her left hand showed her desire for ambition, but on her right it was foreshortened, showing that she had no confidence and was allowing herself to take a back seat. Her left-hand head line sloped creatively and had a business fork at the end revealing her innate business acumen, but on her right hand it moved straight across her palm, ending before the mount of Moon.

Today, those patterns of frustration on her right hand have changed. The muscles and tendons have relaxed to allow the finger of Jupiter to assume its natural position as longer than the finger of Sun. The old head line has begun to fade for the second half of its length and a new, sloping, forked line, strong and full of new energy, has taken its place.

I have observed over and over again that this technique of creating a stage/radio TV scenario works well for many people because it involves media that are up-to-the-minute, universal and the essence of our culture. It works whether you are shy, retiring, a high-flyer, a housewife, a pensioner, ambitious or not. Putting yourself up there on stage or TV extolling your virtues does wonders for making you feel that you are a valuable member of the human race, and it can often uncover hidden ambitions or make you see where you can improve things.

Doris's story

Doris was in her late sixties and widowed. She had been brought up in an era where women were not expected to work for a living, but she had kept an immaculate house and raised four children who had all done well for themselves.

Doris's real purpose in coming to me was in the hope that a new partner might be on the horizon for her. She dreaded spending her advancing years alone. There was a faint, feathery affection line on her left hand, but nothing on her right except lines of dwindling energy.

She was very enthusiastic about these techniques and was conscientious about trying all of them – the ones for prosperity, health and self-esteem, as well as the ones for love. She decided to write a rough draft for the chat-show introduction while she was with me. It read:

'Ladies and gentlemen, our special guest tonight is Doris. Born and bred in Yorkshire, she has brought her native characteristics of honesty, hard work and plain speaking to the raising of her own family of four children . . .'

She didn't go any further. Instead, she just said, 'You know, Jackie, as I look at that, all I can think is, what a bloody wasted life. What I really wanted to do was to be a nurse, but our Stan [her late husband] wouldn't hear of it. Now it's too late.'

I encouraged her to do something about it. Training to be a nurse these days is rigorous and high-powered and Doris felt that she was past it, but through seeing herself as she really wanted to be and by following her intuition, she ended up helping out at a hospice and taking some O-levels, as they then were, in biology and anatomy at a college of further education.

Doris had left school at fourteen with no qualifications at all. Today she is a qualified reflexologist and aromatherapist, and apart from her own private practice offers her services one day a week at a day centre for the elderly. If anyone suggests to her that she ought to be an inmate of the centre rather than a worker there, they get the blunt edge of her Yorkshire tongue.

Her delight in her new prospects took her mind completely off thoughts of love and romance, but she found it anyway. He was a fellow student on her reflexology course. As a result, the feathery affection line on her left hand strengthened and a completely new one developed on her right.

If Doris had remained as she was, living a quiet and isolated life as a widow, the feathery affection line on her hand would probably have remained like that – a line of vague potential. By working on all areas of her life, she enabled her true potential to develop. Now her whole hand has changed. Her head line has strengthened and lengthened, and her lifeline has developed a strong branch that swings away from the old, dwindling line. Instead of fading into poor health, she is moving into a vigorous and energetic new life.

See yourself as the best

Almost unconsciously, so many of us go around saying and thinking things about ourselves that sabotage any ideas or dreams we have, things like:

1. I'm too fat
2. I'm too thin
3. My brain's the size of a pea
4. My memory's going
5. I can't cope
6. It's too much for me
7. I couldn't do that – what would people think?
8. I'd be a laughing stock
9. I haven't enough experience
10. I'm too young
11. I'm too old
12. I'm not good-looking enough
13. I'll do it later
14. I can't do that until I'm older/slimmer . . .

These thoughts sit in our minds, whittling away at our major plans, holding us back, depressing us. Let's change them.

Step 1 Find out just which ideas are your own main negative impulses. You may already have discovered most of them from the other techniques in this book, but just to make sure, take a moment now to check again.

- In what ways do you feel that you aren't good enough?
- What are the things you don't feel you can do?
- What don't you like about yourself?
- What don't you like about your looks?

Step 2   Turn each negative statement into an affirmation. The list on p. 197 would then look like this:

1. Each day I—am slimmer and closer to my ideal weight
2. Each day my figure is more lovely and rounded
3. My brain is a normal size and functions better every day
4. My memory is better every time I use it
5. I—can cope with everything
6. I—can manage and accomplish any task I want
7. I—can do anything I like. Other people respect me
8. Whatever I—do has value. The people I—respect do not laugh at me
9. I have enough experience to do what I—want to do
10. I—am old enough
11. I—am never too old to do whatever I want
12. I—am daily more attractive and desirable
13. I—can do it right now
14. I—can do it at the right time for me. I do not need to wait and I—erase the negative, erroneous thoughts that are holding me back

Step 3   Take a piece of paper and colouring pencils or paints if you have them. Now draw a picture of yourself in a scene that contains all the things you want in your life.

Be completely free about this. If your ideal is being on a tropical island with some gorgeous person practising all the poses of the Karma Sutra, draw this. Yes, draw it. All of it, or until you feel that you've done enough.

If your ideal is to don walking boots and go hiking in the Welsh mountains or the Alps or wherever, draw that.

It doesn't matter if you can't draw very well and your people start out as matchstick men and women. You will improve as you do this, but more importantly it will tap some of the hidden areas of your psyche.

If you've got several ideal scenes and many things you want, you can draw as many pictures as you need.

Your drawings might make you laugh. Mine did, with all these little twiggy stick people cavorting in apparently impossible places doing apparently impossible things. But these pictures also gave me a brilliant sense of exhilaration. A sense of 'Why not?' And that's when things begin to happen, when situations begin to change.

Step 4 Find a photograph of your own head and face. If you can only find full-length shots, cut round your head and use that.

Take a large piece of paper, for example a sheet of sugar paper, or even buy a scrapbook if you like, and paste or tape the picture of your head on to it.

Now start a collection of pictures from magazines or newspapers of all the things you want in your life.

First of all you are going to need a picture of a body for your head. Find one that suits the way you want to look. Perhaps your body is already the way you want it, in which case use a full-length photograph of yourself.

Next, find pictures of people in the types of clothes you want to wear:

- The kind of car you want to drive
- The kind of house you want to live in
- The rooms and furniture
- The kinds of holiday you want to take
- The kind of work environment you want

Paste these pictures on or around your own picture. You may need several pages to fulfil your ideal life.

Remember that this is all about self-esteem and bolstering your self-image. The most important picture is the one of you, so you may need several photographs of yourself.

Find some pictures of people smiling. Cut these out and place them around a picture of you, so that you see yourself surrounded by attractive people smiling at you in an encouraging way.

Step 5 Look at these collages every day for up to

twenty-eight days and say appropriate affirmations, for example:

1. There is nothing to stop me—living like this
2. I—am attractive and charming to everyone I meet
3. Everyone I—meet is bowled over by me
4. I—am beginning this lifestyle right now
5. I—am as good as anyone else living on this planet
6. There is no one quite like me and I—am brilliant and wonderful

If you are working on money and prosperity you might like to draw some sacks of gold with dollar or sterling signs for however many thousands of dollars/pounds you are working towards, and also to say some affirmations around this. Similarly, if you are improving your work life or working on success, you might like to draw yourself in appropriate situations or cut out pictures of stars receiving Oscars or people receiving large prizes or cheques, and insert your own photograph into the scene.

This is your blueprint.

It is essentially what you want or what you want to be, and once your subconscious mind absorbs a visual image of what you are actually aiming for, it will come up with all sorts of odd, unique and surprising ways of getting it to you.

The result is inevitable. Your mind will be on a kind of autopilot, moving you from where you are towards where you want to be.

How long this takes and how many adjustments you need to make depends on you. There will be days and weeks, sometimes even months, when you feel fed up and think it's all a load of rubbish, so that you put things on the back burner. But if you have set your goals, made affirmations and tried some of the other techniques, your subconscious mind won't have forgotten and will often deliver results when you least expect them.

The aim of the next exercise is to give your self-esteem an added boost, and to accelerate you towards your goals.

Giving yourself a day that is completely yours

At least once a month – more often if you can manage it – put a day aside especially for you. It doesn't matter whether you're single or have a partner – *everyone needs to do this*. If you can't manage a day, try half a day or an evening.

This is an opportunity for you to honour yourself, to get in touch with the things that are really important to you, and to create a physical affirmation that you are the most important person in your world and deserve the very best.

Decide that everything you do on this day will be exactly what you want to do. No compromises.

You can play this day two ways:

a. you can make a plan beforehand of what you want to do. This may be necessary if it involves booking tickets or tables at a restaurant

or, and this is more rewarding psychologically

b. you can let the day unfold itself as you move through it, allowing your intuition and feelings to guide you. If attending a concert or a play was part of your intention and you haven't got tickets, either you will find that the concert hall or theatre has had a cancellation or you will move on and do something else that is actually more rewarding.

Probably the most important part of such a day is first thing when you wake up. Even if you haven't made specific plans there are bound to be things that you want to do. Whatever you do, though, don't make a timetable for your day with plans like, 'I want to be in town by 11.00,' because that is putting your left brain, your organising self, in charge and you won't reap the full benefit.

If you have been used to putting your true desires on the back burner for a long time, the chances are that when you wake up the day will stretch ahead of you and you may possibly feel tense. Here you are, a day all to yourself and you *ought* to be happy and free. Instead you are sinking into boredom, or apathy or irritation.

Get into these feelings. They are the real you trying to tell you something. Sit down (if you've already got up), close your eyes and ask yourself, 'Why am I feeling like this?' (You should try to do this every single day from now on – just check in periodically to see how you are feeling and then act on it.)

You may not get an answer straight away, but if you don't, go about your day anyway. An answer will come in some form. Each time you feel low or stuck during the day, ask yourself, 'How am I really feeling? How does my body feel? Any tension anywhere?' Ask your body what it is it wants to tell you.

The answer is usually pretty close to the surface – maybe a relationship is bugging you, your job is driving you up the wall, or you haven't as much money as you'd like. Whatever it is, decide to take steps to change it. *Do something* no matter how small or large. Use some of the techniques in this book if you like, or something you devise yourself. If you are working on some aspect of your life, now is a good time to incorporate techniques such as affirmations and/or visualisations for half an hour or so.

Although this day is 'yours', you may want to spend at least part of it with others. It is important then to be aware of your boundaries. Are you still doing what you really want to do, or is a stronger personality trying to get things going his or her way?

For example, you may meet some friends for a drink and although you really want to see them and to have a chat as part of your day, one of them suggests going to a restaurant where you don't really like the food or the atmosphere.

If you go, you are actually not achieving the purpose of your day. You are honouring your friend, not yourself. This is one time when you should say exactly what you feel. Remember that your aim here is to help yourself over the difficulties that have been holding you back, and to create new directions and fulfilment in your life. You are trying to set your own boundaries, so in such a situation it is a good exercise to say that you don't really like the place and would prefer to go somewhere else. If you are overruled, it is up to you. If you go, you will know that there is a fragile part of you that is frightened of upsetting your friends and that needs people even when they're not sensitive to your needs. You need to learn to value yourself more.

Friendship is always a balancing act of give and take and compromise. What we are talking about here is not friendship per se, but giving yourself a totally free, anything-is-possible day so that you can discover yourself a bit more. Most good friends who know what you're doing will cosset you anyway.

A good example of how friendship can help, and also of how making plans for your day can go both amazingly wrong and in your favour, was demonstrated by a close friend of mine.

She had decided to give herself a fully cosseting Saturday where everything was open to chance except a hair appointment in the morning and tickets for a concert at the Festival Hall in the afternoon. You might say that this was a fairly organised day, but it didn't turn out that way.

She shared a flat in London with two other girls who were both away for the weekend, so she turned off her alarm clock and slept until she woke naturally. She lay in bed savouring the delicious cosiness of being able just to lie there and do nothing.

Then she ran a warm bath and soaked in it while some croissants were warming in the oven. After breakfast, she took the tube to Harrods where she was going to have her hair done and then do some shopping.

She does remember feeling a bit empty at this point. She would have loved a partner to be sharing her day with, especially when she took herself off for a solitary lunch at a restaurant.

It was while she was getting on the tube to go to the concert that two boys jostled her, and when she came out at her station she realised that her purse with her money and concert tickets had gone. The underground staff were helpful, but she was distraught.

In a blind panic she made her way to the flat of a friend who lived nearby, who was very kind and supportive. She also had her brother staying for the weekend. He only came to stay once in a blue moon, and what happened? You've probably guessed: it was mega-electricity between them at first sight, and it blazed away to become a full-blown love affair.

They are happily married now and still muse about the surprising good fortune of that stolen purse.

My friend feels that by trying to give herself her own day she was coming close to what she really wanted, especially when she felt lonely. She feels that her sense of loneliness and her decision to spend a 'happy' day all to herself was actually a physical affirmation and that because of it she attracted those young muggers. Nothing other than a major shock could have diverted her, so that her deepest longings could be fulfilled.

This brings me to an interesting correlation with her affection lines. Her left-hand lines showed that a deep love affair should have started about a year previously, while her right hand showed a rather wavy, pale line, indicating that her love life was currently unsatisfactory. What this meant was that she should have met her husband a year before she actually did – and indeed, there had been several opportunities in the previous year when she could have met him. For various reasons she had turned down two invitations from her friend when he would have been present.

However, when she gave herself her 'day' she had switched off her left-brained, logical, organising self, thereby allowing her natural path to develop on its own.

The Last Word

As a baby you were demanding, powerful and uncivilised.

Dare to reclaim some of that vital force. In your imagination dare to remember, to take yourself back to that energy. Make contact with it and learn to use it with control.

10

Putting It All Together

Life is lived minute by minute. The most important experience we can have is right now. At this minute, you are reading this, so take a moment to check how you feel. Is the air warm on your body? Does your head feel clear? Are your limbs comfortable?

This is you in all your wonderful complexity, and ticking away in your consciousness are those desires that will lead to greater expansion and fulfilment. They are with you constantly and it is on a daily basis that we can begin to move forward little by little, creating and attracting results. Use the following programme to help you.

Creating a Daily Programme

It doesn't matter if you are concentrating on just one area of your life like health or prosperity, or if you are really going for it right across the board with love, health, prosperity, self-esteem and work, the following is a suggestion for a daily programme.

Be aware of how you feel

On waking, either write a few affirmations or sit and be aware of your feelings. If you are feeling heavy, gently move your awareness into it to see what has caused it. It may be a relationship or work, or it may be a general feeling of lassitude. Be aware of this, because it is something that you have to deal with. If you know that there is something you can do about it today, then make a mental, or even actual, note to do it. Otherwise, be aware that the difficulty is there but concentrate on the things that you are working on. You will probably find that the heaviness you have been feeling will surface quite naturally in your techniques and that you can sort it out then.

Practise visualisation and passive exercises

Set aside fifteen to twenty minutes when you will be undisturbed. It doesn't matter what time of day you choose, but you should try to do this at least once a week, though if you enjoy it, every day would be ideal.

Decide the main area you want to work on – your wildest dream, your health, weight, body, finances etc – and then use the exercise given in Chapter 5 to reach the alpha brain-wave rhythm. Stay in this relaxed state for a few minutes and give yourself a health boost by sending energy to your glands and cells (see pp. 99–103). Now use any of the techniques given for the particular area you are working on, for example creative visualisation for prosperity, love or work, or affirmations, which should be said mentally. When you have done this, you can then include any other areas you are working on to pep them up.

At the end of every session, make contact with your intuitive self by taking your awareness down to your abdominal area and ask your body what you need to know, or what you need to be doing.

You can ask specific questions, especially if you are stuck about something. Either you will get an immediate answer, or you will find that your mood lifts or changes automatically over the next day or so.

If you have made a tape and don't feel like a meditative exercise, listen to that instead. A lot of people listen to their tapes in the car, which is a good way of saving time provided that they don't distract you.

Keep checking how you feel

During the day, check in periodically to see how you are feeling. Are you happy? Uneasy? Is someone bothering you? Maybe someone has asked you to do something or go somewhere and you don't want to. Practise pleasing yourself. Whatever your feelings are telling you, check them out. They are your true self trying to break free of the constraints you have applied.

If it feels too scary to tell your friend or colleague that you can't do what he or she wants, be aware of your fear and realise that it has been running your life. Realise that you have been choosing to go with the fear rather than feel relaxed and happy doing what you want to do. Try to do some small thing to release yourself from it. Practise saying 'No' when you really don't want to fit in with someone else, saying it gently and with a smile. Use the exercises for self-esteem (see pp. 186–204) and for health and weight (see pp. 143–145), which will help to get you in touch with your fears.

Write a list of ten things you love doing, whether it's having a shower and plastering yourself with body lotion, eating pizza, or whatever. Make sure you do at least one or more of the things on your list *every* single day.

Write a new list every month. It may be the same or slightly different, but continue doing at least one of the items on it, preferably more, every day.

Get an attractive notebook for writing down your goals and affirmations. I have a pretty file into which I put A4 lined paper in assorted colours. Also, every so often, especially on my birthday and other important days, I buy myself a greetings card, write in it my current favourite affirmations, and then prop it up where I can enjoy it for a week or so.

Review your day

Last thing at night, look back on your day and see where you could have improved things. Give yourself a pat on the

back for what you have achieved and programme yourself
for a good night's sleep by affirming to yourself that your
body will take all the rest and nourishing sleep it needs.

If you have a partner all this can go out of the window
despite your good intentions, so do it in the bathroom after
you've cleaned your teeth, or when you are having a bath
or shower.

Above all, if you forget – and we all do, sometimes for
weeks or even months at a time – it doesn't matter a jot.
When you're ready you will get back to it. Just know that
whenever you choose to do these things for yourself this
is the right time for you to be doing them, and whatever
you are choosing to work on is the best thing for you.

You are in charge of your life, no one else. If you have
made a few mistakes, that's fine. We all do. You are still
in charge and you can do what it takes to correct them.

Review your goals

Every so often review where you are with your goals and
make some larger affirmations, like taking that holiday,
buying that new outfit, eating in that new restaurant.

If you feel that your goals are not being achieved, use
the technique of contacting your intuition described on
side 2 of the tape. Ask yourself what you need to do to
achieve what you want. It may be that you need to make
a few adjustments in order to bring yourself into the right
frame of mind for achieving your goals.

Above all, as you work with these exercises, you will
see that the clearer your mind becomes, the sooner you
will realise what it is you want, and the more you practise
the techniques, the clearer your mind will be. In other
words, practice brings results, and the patterns on your
hands will gradually change to reflect this.

But don't expect monumental change in a short space
of time. Your main lines of life, head and heart will
still be there. What you will notice is a lengthening,
deepening or even a change of direction, or new lines
of direction replacing the old. Your fingers may fill out

to show improvements in prosperity and self-esteem. The colour and 'feel' of your palms may change to show a more dynamic life force being allowed to flow.

As I said at the beginning, your hands mirror your life showing you where you are now in your life and where you will be going unless you change your thoughts. Change your thoughts and you can change your direction and your destination.

It is *completely* under your control.

So have fun with it all. Love your life, your work, your friends, your exercises, and watch yourself steadily achieve everything you ever wanted . . .

Appendix

Suggested Further Reading

David Brandon-Jones, *The Art of Hand Analysis*.
Gabriel Cousens, MD, *Spiritual Nutrition and the Rainbow Diet*.
Shakti Gawain, *Living in the Light*.
Gerry Gillies, *Moneylove*.
—— *Psychological Immortality*.
Louise Hay, *You Can Heal Your Life*.
Phil Laut, *Money is my Friend*.
Catherine Ponder, *The Dynamic Laws of Prosperity*.
Sondra Ray, *How To Be Chic, Fabulous and Live Forever*.
Sondra Ray and Leonard Orr, *Rebirthing in the New Age*.
Baird Spalding, *Life and Teaching of the Masters of the Far East*.
Stuart Wilde, *The Trick to Money is Having Some*.
—— *The Force*.
—— *Miracles*.

Useful Addresses

Transcendental Meditation

National Communications Office,
Beacon House,
Willow Walk,
Woodley Park,
Skelmersdale,
Lancashire
Freefone: 0800 269 303

Chiropractors

McTimoney Chiropractic Association,
21 High Street,
Eynsham,
Oxford OX8 1HE

Reflexology

The British Reflexology Association
Monks Orchard
Whitbourne
Worcester
WR6 5RB

*Bach flower remedies, homeopathic remedies,
alternative therapies (mail order)*

Neal's Yard Apothecary,
5 Golden Cross Walk,
Cornmarket Street,
Oxford
Tel: (0865) 245436

Rebirthing (general enquiries)

Gilly Montgomery,
5 Manor Road,
Catcott,
Bridgewater,
Somerset TA7 9HT
Tel: (0278) 722536

Bookshops

Watkins Books Ltd,
19 Cecil Court,
London WC2N 4EZ
Tel: (071) 836 2182

Mysteries,
9–11 Monmouth Street,
London WC2H 9DA
Tel: (071) 240 3688

The Inner Bookshop,
111 Magdalen Road,
Oxford
Tel: (0865) 245301